THE NEW LANDSCAPE
URBANISATION IN THE THIRD WORLD

THE NEW LANDSCAPE

URBANISATION IN THE THIRD WORLD

Charles Correa

A Mimar Book

Butterworth Architecture

A Mimar Book published by Concept Media Ltd. with
Butterworth Architecture, an imprint of Butterworth Scientific

 PART OF REED INTERNATIONAL P.L.C.

ISBN 0-408-50071-9 Published by Butterworth Architecture
in North America, Europe (West and East, excluding all of
Turkey), South Africa, Australia and New Zealand.

ISBN 9971-84-868-6 Published by Concept Media elsewhere,
except USSR and India.

Design by Viscom Design Associates, Singapore
Printed by Oversea Printing Suppilies Pte Ltd, Singapore

All photographs and drawings courtesy of the author,
except for those listed on page 120.

For Monika

who always encouraged me to go
in this direction…with the sneaking
suspicion that these thoughts and
ideas, however inadequately
expressed, are more relevant to our
world than any buildings I could
ever possibly build.

AUTHOR'S NOTE

I must first of all thank my daughter, Chinu, for the inexhaustible enthusiasm and care she brought to the task of getting this material together – words, photographs and sketches. And to Hasan, who has guided with much care and patience the making of this MIMAR edition. So also to Valerie, who typed out the manuscript – many many times – with the zeal of the true believer. And to all at Concept Media and Viscom in Singapore – especially Pat and Sylvia. And to the photographers for the use of their pictures, in particular Joseph St. Anne whose unforgettable mythic image of Bombay ends the book.

This book does not presume to deal with all the issues of urbanisation in the Third World. Far from it. I have merely tried to set down those pieces of the new landscape which have begun to surface in the course of my experiences – both here in Bombay, as well as in other cities of this sub-continent. There is no doubt in my mind that this rapid urbanisation (triggered off by tidal waves of distress migration) is going to be the crucial — economic, political and moral — issue of the next three decades. Yet, surprisingly enough, there does not exist today a theoretical schema which can provide a basis for coherent action. The conceptualisation of such a schema must be given the highest priority. And it will have to be done by those who are involved, day after day, in the issues – just as the great theoreticians of guerilla warfare were not academics, but the ones that did the actual fighting: Mao Tse-Tung and Che Guevara.

One last point. Throughout this text I have used the term: the Third World. I find this far better than those miserable (and inaccurate) euphemisms; "under-developed" and/or "developing". "The Third World", as most of us know, was a phrase coined in the 1950's by Nehru. Tito, Nasser and other leaders of the Non-aligned movement, in order to define a third option, one different from Joseph Stalin's USSR and John Foster Dulles USA. It is precisely this third choice that I wish to draw to your attention.

Bombay, 1988

CONTENTS

Introduction

Across the globe, the towns and cities of the Third World are growing very rapidly. In most Third World countries, the annual population growth rate is somewhere between 2 to 3%, but the towns and cities themselves are increasing at more than double this speed. This growth is compounded by the great waves of distress migration from the rural areas where farmlands cannot sustain the population. And so people flee to the cities and become squatters, living illegally on pavements or in whatever crevices they can find.

Migrants, Rosso, Mauritania.

This is the most spectacular growth rate of all. Consider the case of Bombay. Twenty years ago there were fewer than 400,000 squatters in a population of 4.5 million. Today there are almost 4.5 million in a population of 9 million. Thus while the nation has grown by 50% and the city by 100%, the squatters have increased more than 1100%! Facts such as these are going to change the images triggered in our minds by the word "city".

Today, of the dozen giant metropolii of 10 million plus, the best known — New York, London, Tokyo, Los Angeles — are in rich

Urbanscape, U.S.A.

industrialised countries. Thus the word "city" conveys clearly-defined icons: high-rise towers, automobiles and clover leafs, and so forth.

Yet, quite soon, by the year 2000, there will be about 50 cities of 15 million around the globe — of which more than 40 will be in the Third World! Most of these are cities whose images are foggy in the extreme — if *any* image at all is conjured up by the sound of their names: Dhaka, Jakarta, Bombay, Canton. Like the Tonda region of Manila, they evoke in your mind, one suspects, an amorphous undifferentiated mass of humanity, on cycles and on foot, clogging the roads in all directions. Just as the icon of the mushroom cloud has dominated our consciousness in the last four decades, so this new urban image will determine the moral issues of the next century.

Obviously, the migrants in these cities have their own priorities. As a Latin-American friend, concerned with family planning, says: "How do you tell a poor Mexican farmer that if he has ten children, the world will end in disaster, when he already lives with disaster?" In any case, our concern about the fate of humanity in the coming Apocalypse is perhaps a selfish one. We are worried

Icon of the 20th Century . . .

. . . and of the 21st.

The human condition: "Bicycle thieves" by De Sica.

about whether we ourselves can live through the holocaust without our usual life-support systems. The poor can easily survive with nothing. As they are doing right now.

The resilience and inventiveness of humanity is truly incredible. A few years ago, I saw some of those neo-realist films produced by Italy in the immediate aftermath of World War II. They were a revelation. *Shoeshine, Bicycle Thieves, Open City*: these depict the lives of millions and millions of people in cities all over the Third World today. In fact, a film like *Bicycle Thieves* could be shot in any one of a hundred Asian cities — Bangkok, Poona, Jakarta — with hardly any change. For not only did the Italy of that heroic post-war period single-handedly invent much of the hardware (the motor-scooter, for instance) which today dominates our Third World cities, it also embodied the essential socio-political equation: family-oriented people facing up to the brutal crunch of a new industrial economy and surviving with — and because of — their humanity. To me, the Italy of that period is the proto-typical developing country, as relevant to the people of the Third World as Mahatma Gandhi's India or Mao's China.

The year 2000 is not so far away. It's closer in fact, than 1975. And, as we approach the start of the next century, one begins to suspect that the cities of the Third World could, perhaps, pull through. Fragments of the future, like pieces of a jig-saw puzzle, are surfacing more and more frequently. Slowly, inexorably, they are beginning to generate a new landscape.

1

Urbanisation

Sharing a cup of tea. Note the excellent location — flanked by public transport.

Very often we fail to recognise fragments of the new landscape because our view of the Third World is both limited and egocentric. Consider, for instance, one of the most miraculous and largely uncelebrated characteristics of the Third World. Despite poverty and exploitation, despite centuries of deprivation, the people — as social and human entities — are still largely intact. This is a factor of crucial importance to their development. Although in the eyes of the well-to-do citizen the squatter struggling to shelter his family may be seen as an anti-social element, from any other point of view his endeavour is as marvellous, intuitive and socially positive as a bird building a nest. Compare the phenomenon he represents with the muggings and meaningless slayings of most North American cities.

But will these characteristics — this innate decency which takes centuries to create, and which presumably is one of the main fall-outs of that process we call civilisation — survive the jolting demographic changes that are taking place? For in most of the Third World, urban centres are growing about twice as fast as overall population.

This tidal flow of population is not, of course, due merely to the pull of big city lights. Most of it is distress migration from the

Population in Millions

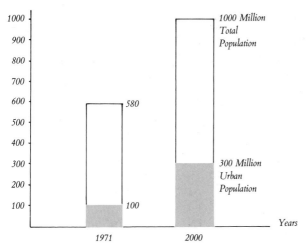

1000 Million
Total
Population

580

300 Million
Urban
Population

100

Years

1971   2000

India, for instance, is today a country of 771 million, of which 177 million people (i.e. 23%) are urban dwellers — which means that India, a predominantly rural nation, already has an urban population almost the same size of that in the U.S.A.
While the overall population is growing at 2.2%., the urban sector is increasing much faster, at over 4%. Demographers estimate that by the year 2030 the birth rate will level off, and the population will stabilise at about 1620 million people — by which time, as many as 600 million would be urban dwellers. Thus, the urban sector will increase four-fold-in absolute terms, an increase of 450 million urban dwellers.

villages to the urban centres by marginal earners (landless labour, etc.) whose existence can no longer be sustained by the rural areas. These desperately poor migrants come to towns and cities to look for work. Housing has a very low priority on their list of needs. They want to be where the jobs are. Hence their willing acceptance of life in crevices of the city, as illegal squatters and pavement dwellers. To offer them self-help housing on land at the edge of the city, far away from the jobs, is to misunderstand totally their predicament. This is why the migrants (at least the smart ones) move back on to the pavements, as near as possible to where they can find work.

Any solution to distress migration will necessarily be complex, and will include several facets. First of all, land redistribution and social reform must be implemented in the villages so as to increase

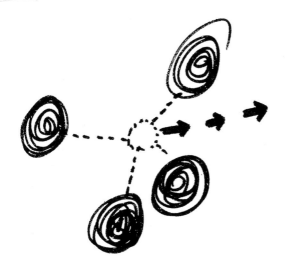

Village cluster growth: New employment (cottage industries, etc.) and social infrastructure (a health centre, a school) located centrally to a cluster of villages. Inhabitants continue to use existing stock of housing until the whole cluster gradually coalesces into a new growth centre. This would also allow the rationalisation of the transport system: cycle and bullock-cart from village to new centre, buses between centres, etc. all the way up to trains and aeroplanes connecting the large metropolii.

17

*India: medium size cities are growing
faster than large metropolii.*

India: medium size cities are gr
faster than large metropolii.
One million and above
100,000 to one million

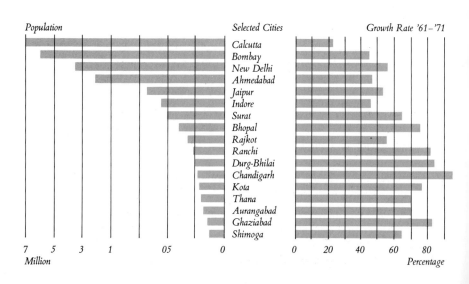

Population	Selected Cities	Growth Rate '61–'71
	Calcutta	
	Bombay	
	New Delhi	
	Ahmedabad	
	Jaipur	
	Indore	
	Surat	
	Bhopal	
	Rajkot	
	Ranchi	
	Durg-Bhilai	
	Chandigarh	
	Kota	
	Thana	
	Aurangabad	
	Ghaziabad	
	Shimoga	

7   5   3   1   05   0
Million

0   20   40   60   80
Percentage

their holding capacity. Secondly, key market towns in each district must be identified and reinforced with appropriate investments so that they become new growth centres. Thirdly, all new industry and major offices (including government ones) should be located in small and middle-sized cities, not in the large metropolii.

The first objective, land redistribution and social reform, is the most crucial task of all. It is what Mahatma Gandhi was trying to bring about through his village development programmes (*khadi*, cloth-spinning, etc.) and what Mao so spectacularly accomplished for China through his communes. In most cases, it will involve a redistribution of land holdings — as for instance in India, where so many of the urban migrants are destitute landless labour. This means changes in the class/caste structure — perhaps the most difficult political objective of all. Yet, if that is not done, developmental funds and resources (i.e. irrigation schemes, government loans, etc.) get routed through the rural elite — who use it to increase their own leverage, thus triggering off even more distress migration.

The other two objectives are more easily achieved. Because of national policies regarding industrial location and financial investments, the largest cities in India are not the fastest-growing. Bombay and Calcutta are increasing at a little over 4% annually, whereas medium-sized cities such as Bangalore and Bhopal are growing at more than 7%.

If these objectives are attained, then Bombay, which today has 9 million citizens, may stabilise at 15 million or so. If not, then Bombay will go the way of Mexico City which by the turn of the century is expected to shelter 30 million inhabitants. Actually, Mexico has an advantage over India. Its total population is only 55 million, so there is an upper limit to how large its cities can become. India's population — and our urban future — is far more open-ended.

To the industrialised West, numbers like these are traumatic, yet the trauma cannot be resolved unless we understand that functionally these migrations serve to readjust socio-economic pressures. Thus, far from being an indicator of the demise of a people, they are a sign of hope, of the will to survive. In fact wouldn't India be a far more pessimistic proposition if the have-nots just lay down in the villages, waiting to die?

In any case, mass migration to urban areas is not a new phenomenon. European populations grew several fold between the 17th and 19th centuries, and were equally foot-loose for much the same reasons: growing rural population, limited supply of arable land, and so forth. That precedent, however, had one crucial difference. The Europeans did not need to readjust themselves

The will to survive.

within their own national boundaries. Because of their military clout they were able to distribute themselves around the globe – which in turn led to higher standards of living, and hence to smaller families. (Family planning is an automatic result of rising expectations, not vice versa. People do not have smaller families for altruistic, "national" reasons – nor larger ones, as witness the futile attempts of successive French and German governments to raise their countries' birthrates.)

Trying to influence family size — and failing.

Unfortunately, this kind of global redistribution is not an option for the Third World today — certainly not to India or any other Asian country. To understand this is to begin to perceive the crucial role which our towns and cities are actually playing. They are substitutes for migrating to Australia; functioning, in effect, as mechanisms for generating employment. How, then, can we increase their absorptive capacities? There is a limit to the number of jobs which can be generated in industry. The vast majority of migrants to the cities will have to find work in tertiary and bazaar activities. *Any intervention we make on the urban scene, therefore, should aim to increase economic activity in these areas.*

To achieve this, the physical form of the city itself can be of importance. For instance large high-rise buildings restrict activity to the handful of developers who can organise the finance needed for such projects, to the very few engineers and architects who can design the structures, and to the even fewer construction companies that build them — not to mention the profits, much of which go to the banks which underwrite the deals. Compare this to the kind of development we find in old city centres throughout the Third World: small, tightly-packed buildings, each 4 or

Restrictive monopolies: high rise building.

Low-rise, high-density built form: generating jobs in the bazaar.

5 storeys high. With this pattern of development, employment opportunity is spread through the bazaar sector, among masons, carpenters, petty contractors and so forth. Thus the investment spreads the benefits to a much wider segment of the population.

Sadly, these issues are not perceived by the decision-makers and the privileged. Instead, as the migrants pour in, they opt for edicts to stop the tide. Many believe that some kind of permit system to enter the city must be made mandatory, totally ignoring the fact that such measures, apart from trampling on fundamental human rights, are also of questionable morality. What we are saying to the poor is, in effect, "I got here first". Furthermore, far from solving the problem, they only increase political favouritism and bureaucratic corruption.

Squatters in Bombay along the railway tracks — so that they can get to work.

At the other extreme, there are those who would like to legalise all squatter settlements, exactly as is, where is. This approach has the advantage of having a humane and moral basis, but it ignores the *scale* of the phenomenon we are facing. For although it is a fact that a large number of people have managed to find unprotected land and pavements on which to live in various parts of the city, there simply aren't enough such crevices left in most cities for this to be a general solution to the problem.

If Bombay, for instance, had 4 million well-housed inhabitants and no more than 100,000 destitute, then this approach might be valid. There are, however, by government count, 4.5 million illegal squatters in Bombay, with more coming every day. When all the *maidans* (i.e. green areas), and all the staircases of all the buildings are full, where will the people go then?

Obviously more urban land must be generated at a rate and on a scale commensurate with need, and the need is not just for any land anywhere, but land serviced by public *transport* and related to *work opportunities* — in other words, new growth centres which re-adjust the pressure points in the existing city structure.

This approach is perhaps the only way we can urbanise within the implacable financial constraints prevailing in our countries. For in India or Pakistan or Bangladesh, the income per family is extremely low. Using brick and concrete, very little can be constructed within the family budget. In Bombay, the average for almost 30% of the population is somewhere between 1.5 and 3 square metres per family.

Simple mud and bamboo houses built in self-help schemes are very much cheaper; but here the cost of desirable urban land

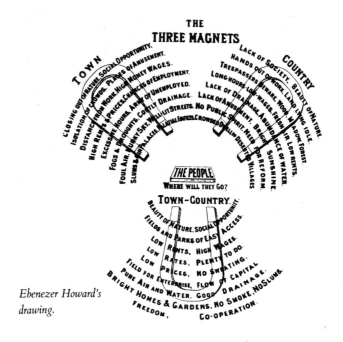

Ebenezer Howard's drawing.

becomes exorbitant. Thus these "sites-and-services" schemes tend to be located, almost without exception, on unwanted land at the edge of the city: a miserable location far away from mass transport lines and hence from employment. At best, many of these schemes become ghettos of cheap labour at the mercy of one or two local factories, perhaps explaining their new-found respectability with the financial establishment.

On the other hand, there are advocates of high-rise housing schemes, as those found in Hong Kong and Singapore. Here the cost of service infrastructure, including mass transport, is lower. Singapore, however, has a per capita income several times higher than Bombay, and the cost of a housing unit in a multi-storey building is far beyond the reach of most Third World poor. And if any subsidies are available, they are subject to many more urgent competing priorities, such as food, health, education and so forth.

So long as we deal only with small bits and pieces of the problem, there does not seem to be any solution in sight. To find the new landscape, we must start with an overview; we must examine the *entire* system we call "city" and try to identify those living patterns, those life-styles, which are optimal in their totality — including roads, services, schools, transportation systems, social facilities and, of course, the housing units themselves. Only then will we be able to perceive how one can, in Buckminister Fuller's ineffable phrase "rearrange the scenery".

High-rise housing in Hong Kong.

This is, in fact, the opportunity of New Bombay, a growth centre for 2 million people currently being developed across the harbour from the old city. It is an attempt to divert the office jobs (which in Bombay are growing three times as fast as industrial jobs) away from the city, so that in one stroke the pressure on the existing city centre is relieved and a key input is added to the urban growth equation across the harbour.

Bombay's growth has been typical of many of the primate cities of the Third World. It took 40 years, from 1900 to 1940, to go from less than 1 million to 1.8 million. With World War II came a jump in population. By 1960, the population had passed the 4 million mark. Today it is over 9 million.

Bombay is not an isolated phenomenon. A number of cities around the world are growing at this rate. For instance, between 1950 and 1986 Abidjan has grown from 69,000 to over a million; Lagos from under 250,000 to over 2 million; Bangkok from less than 1 million to more than 4 million; and Bogota from 650,000 to over 3 million.

Most Third World primate cities (Calcutta, Lima, Hong Kong, etc.) came into being as an interface between colonial powers and the hinterland. The colonials developed them for their own ends – on a scale and with an economic and physical structure that suited their purpose.

After independence, these cities entered a period of rapid growth with no upper limit in sight. In most cases, the new national governments have paid little or no attention to adjusting the obsolete city-structures. Hence, their holding capacity has no relation to the scale of the demands being made on them.

This is particularly true of Bombay. Like many other seaports, the city is one long breakwater protecting the harbour from the open sea. The East India Company started the settlement more

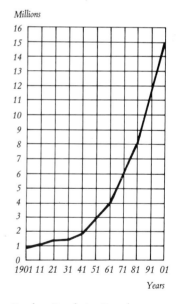

Bombay: Population Growth

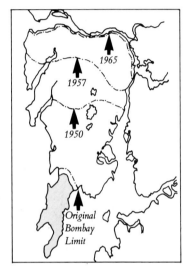

Bombay: Municipal Limits

Heavy road traffic . . .

. . . and overcrowded trains.

than three centuries ago, placing the docks and the fort (i.e. the protected manufacturing and trading area) at the southern tip of this breakwater, right where the ships berthed. The resulting linear structure provided a natural functional framework which sufficed, after a fashion, right up to World War II. Subsequent population increases, however, have stretched this structure further and further, until now, like a rubber band, it is ready to snap.

At the southernmost tip of the island lies an enormous complex of governmental and commercial offices which forms the principle financial centre of India. The office jobs located here, together with the vast textile mills next to them, trigger massive flows of traffic, southward in the morning, northward in the evening. To avoid a gruelling commute of up to 1½ hours each way, people try to live as close as possible to the southern end — in squatter settlements or in over-crowded slums, 10 to 15 in a room.

There is indeed a brutal mismatch between the city's structure and the load it must carry today. As the population escalates, competition for the same facilities increases. And of course the rich win out, pre-empting desirable urban land. Compare the pattern of job locations in the city with land prices. Is it any wonder that the poor sleep out on the pavements?

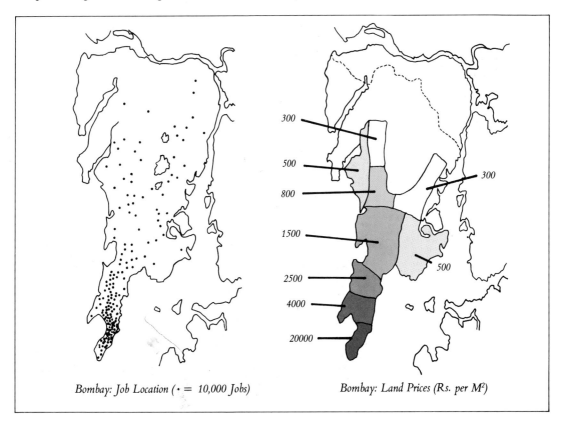

Bombay: Job Location (• = 10,000 Jobs)   *Bombay: Land Prices (Rs. per M²)*

Without doubt, the holding capacity of Bombay must be drastically increased. This was the basis of proposals made to the Government by two colleagues, Pravina Mehta and Shirish Patel, and myself in 1964. In essence, we suggested opening up new growth centres across the harbour so that Bombay's north-south linear structure could change to a circular poly-centred one, making Bombay again what it originally was — that finest of things — a city on the water. In the centre of the whole system: the island caves of Elephanta — an umbilical cord that takes one back a thousand years.

A number of significant but as yet unrelated locational decisions had already been taken unilaterally, involving highways, bridges, industry, and other crucial ingredients of the urban growth equation. We argued that were the authorities to act decisively and add the governmental/commercial function, they might well be able, through the interaction of these inputs, to generate new urban centres on a scale commensurate with Bombay's growth. Furthermore, with public ownership of the land, a cash flow could be set up using the enhanced value of developed acreage to help finance service infrastructure, public transport and housing for the poor. Generating a new pattern of jobs and re-deploying some existing ones could also change "desire lines" across the city, optimising the load on the existing transport network. In short, we were trying to use Bombay's future growth to restructure the city.

Elephanta caves: in the centre of Bombay harbour.

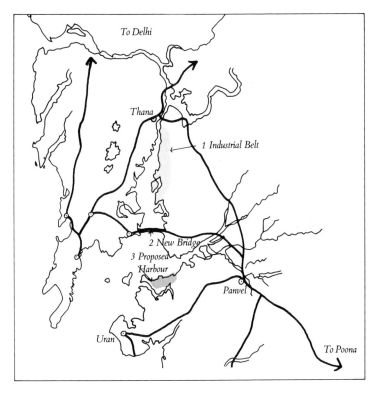

Bombay: Before CIDCO

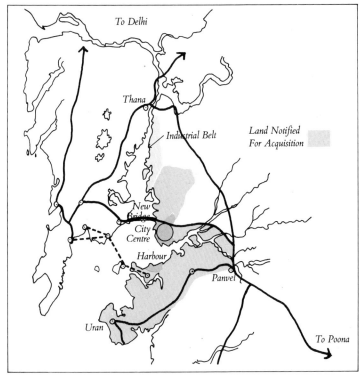

Bombay: After CIDCO

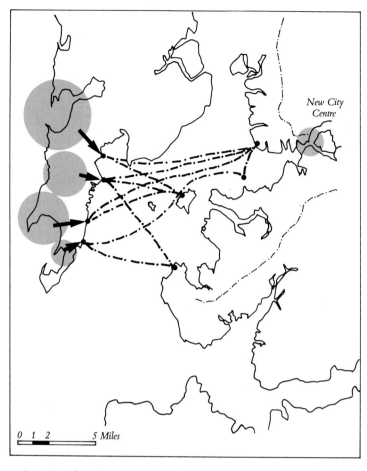

New City
Centre

0 1 2   5 Miles

Re-structuring the city.

In 1970 the Government of Maharashtra accepted the basic planning concepts and notified 55,000 acres of land for acquisition. It set up the City and Industrial Development Corporation — CIDCO — to design and develop the new city called New Bombay. Since the metropolitan region was expected to grow by about 4 million between 1970 and 1985, it was estimated that about half (2 million) would live in the new city.

In such a venture, and with such an opportunity, how does one rearrange the scenery?

2

Space as
a Resource

Early morning in the city.

Visiting a city like Bombay or Calcutta, the first thing that strikes one is the poverty all around. This urban poverty is perhaps the worst pollution of all. Way before you see smoke in the sky or smell sulphur in the air, you see people all around, living and dying on the pavements. Is it inevitable that poverty should degrade life in this manner?

In rural India the poverty has a far different expression. The people are just as poor, perhaps even poorer, but they are not so dehumanised. In the village environment there is always space to meet and talk, to cook, to wash clothes. There is always a place

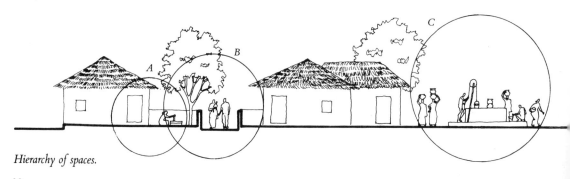

Hierarchy of spaces.

for the children to play. Need we take a look at how these same activities occur in our cities? Obviously, there is no relation between the way our cities have been built and the way people have to use them.

Urban living involves much more than just the use of a small room of, say, 10 square metres. The room, the cell, is only one element in a whole system of spaces that people need.

This system is generally hierarchial. For us, under Indian conditions, it appears to have four major elements:

First, space needed by the family for private use, such as cooking, sleeping and storage;

Second, areas of intimate contact, such as the front doorstep where children play and adults chat with their neighbours;

Third, neighbourhood meeting places, such as the city watertap or village well, where people interact and become a part of community;

And fourth, the principal urban area, such as the *maidan*, used by the whole city.

In different societies the number of elements and their inter-relations may vary, but all human settlements throughout the world — from the tiny hill towns of Italy to the sprawling metropolii of London or Tokyo — have some analogue of such a system; an analogue which modulates with climate, income levels, cultural patterns, etc. of the society concerned.

There are two important facts about the workings of these systems. The first is that each element consists of both covered spaces and open-to-sky spaces. This fact is of fundamental significance because most developing countries are in tropical climates where essential activities can and do take place outdoors. Provided of course, that privacy is reasonably assured, cooking, sleeping, entertaining friends, children's play, etc. need not be exclusively indoor activities, but can function effectively in an open courtyard. In Bombay, for instance, we estimate that at least 75% of essential functions of living can occur in an open-to-sky space. Since the monsoon lasts only 3 months, this is true for 70%

A: Courtyard

B: Doorstep

C: Water tap

D: Community space

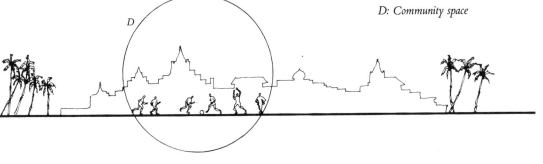

Village council in Senegal.

Town centre in Nepal.

Intelligent built-form.

of the year. Thus open-to-sky space has a *usability coefficient* of about half (i.e. .75 × .70) that of a built-up room. Similarly, we can estimate the usability coefficients of the other built-form conditions — verandahs, pergola-covered terraces, even tree-shaded courtyards — that lie in the spectrum between the enclosed room and open-to-sky space.

Now, just as they have usability coefficients, each of these spaces *Fatehpur-Sikri, Agra.* also has a *production cost*: brick and cement in the case of a room, urban land (and hence longer service infrastructure lines) in the case of a courtyard. The point of trade-off between these variables determines the optimal pattern and density of housing at any particular location. In the Third World today there are countless examples of marvellously innovative habitat, from the Casbah in Algiers to the paper houses of Tokyo. Each is an adroit trade-off between the usability coefficient of these various kinds of spaces on the one hand, and their production cost on the other.

The second important fact about this system of hierarchies is that the elements are mutually interdependent. That is to say, a lack of space in one category can be adjusted by providing more in one of the others. For example smaller dwelling units may be compensated by larger community spaces, and vice versa. Sometimes there are glaring imbalances: public open spaces in Delhi, for instance, follow the usual norm of 1.5 hectare per 1000 persons, which works out to about 75 square metres of public open space per family. But what a staggering difference could have been made to the improvement in quality of life for families in the packed hovels of Old Delhi, had even just a fraction of this public space, (now mostly squandered in the monumental vistas and parks of New Delhi), been traded off as a small courtyard for each family.

To identify this hierarchial system, and to understand the nature of these trade-offs, is, of course the first essential step towards providing viable housing. Without it, one is in grave danger of formulating the wrong questions. This misunderstanding is the reason why so many attempts at low-cost housing perceive it only as a simplistic issue of trying to pile up as many dwelling units, (as many cells) as possible on a given site, without any concern for the other spaces involved in the hierarchy. The result: environments which are inhuman, uneconomical – and quite unusable. Their planners have ignored the fundamental principle, namely, that in a warm climate – like cement, like steel – *space itself is a resource.*

Open space in New Delhi . . .

The wrong question . . . (housing in Brazilia).

. . . at the expense of squalor in the old city.

The perfect trade-off between covered and open-to-sky space: the hillside town of Saana, Yemen.

A courtyard in Marrakesh, Morocco.

In using open-to-sky spaces, the territorial privacy of families is of decisive importance, for as the surrounding buildings get taller, these spaces become more and more restricted in function. A ground-floor courtyard can be used by a family for many purposes, including sleeping at night. Two storeys, and one can still cook in it. Five storeys and it's only for children to play in; ten storeys, it's a parking lot. The old indicators of so many square metres of open space per 1000 persons are too simplistic and crude to be useful. We must *disaggregate* these numbers, both qualitatively and quantitatively.

E stimating accurately the production cost of these various spaces (rooms, courtyards, verandahs, etc.) involves examining the relation between building heights and overall densities, since the latter is a key determinant of infrastructure costs on the city scale. This relationship depends on a number of factors, including the size of the housing unit the community space per family. For Indian urban conditions (i.e. an average housing unit of 25 square metres and a community area of about 30 square metres per family for health centres, etc.), we find that ground-floor housing can accommodate about 125 families per hectare, each on a plot 44 square metres in area. Five-storey walk-up apartments double this figure to about 250 families; 20-storey buildings double it again to about 500 families. Thus as the building heights increase *twenty*-fold, gross neighbourhood densities increase only about *four*-fold.

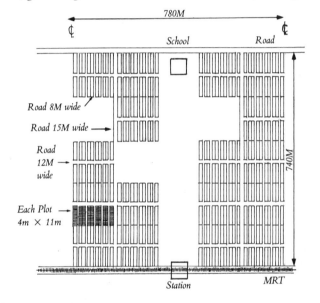

A diagramatic study for a housing sector.

Medium-rise buildings, 30 feet deep. If they fell flat on their faces (where they belong), it would produce wonderful low-rise housing 30 feet high.

And if we step back to see the larger context of the overall city, these variations in density become even less pronounced. For contrary to popular belief, doubling building heights does not save drastically on the overall area of a city. Only about a third of a city is used for housing; the rest is for amenities like industry, transport, green areas, and educational institutions. Furthermore, if we calculate the housing sital area itself, (i.e. the housing sites *without neighbourhood roads, etc.*) then we find that the percentage of land-use devoted to housing sites is usually only about 20%.

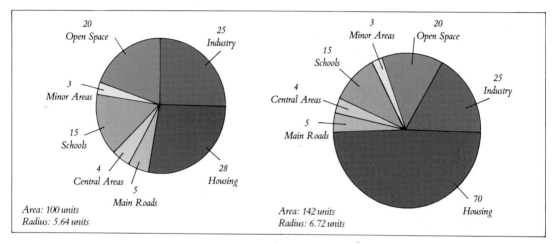

20
Open Space

25
Industry

3
Minor Areas

15
Schools

4
Central Areas

5
Main Roads

28
Housing

Area: 100 units
Radius: 5.64 units

3
Minor Areas

20
Open Space

15
Schools

25
Industry

4
Central Areas

5
Main Roads

70
Housing

Area: 142 units
Radius: 6.72 units

Comparing land-use allocations for Hook New Town, U.K.

Studies undertaken three decades ago for Hook New Town in the U.K. demonstrated that for a circular town, reducing residential densities from 250 persons per hectare to 100 persons per hectare increases the area of the circle by 42%, and the radius — the distance from periphery to city centre — by only 19%. This principle is important even in cold climates, but in the context of the warm climates prevailing in the Third World, such variations in residential densities can cause crucial mutations in the living patterns — really the *life-styles* — of the people. In exchange for only marginal decreases in overall city size, they drastically reduce the open-to-sky space and hence, in our climates, the *usability* of the housing.

Furthermore, these variations dramatically affect the cost of construction. For in a warm climate, shelter can be made from a wide variety of simple materials, ranging from mud and bamboo to sun-dried brick. These constructions are of necessity low-rise. As they go taller, to four-storey walk-ups and higher, the construction has to change to steel or concrete, not because the climate demands it, but for *structural* strength. The resulting escalation in cost is enormous. In contrast, in the cold climates of Europe and North America, variations in construction costs (as a function of building height) have a much narrower range, since even a

Shelter: materials chosen for economy/comfort . . .

. . . and for structural strength.

ground-floor house must be constructed of relatively expensive thermally-insulated materials.

By "low-rise" one means not only self-help housing, but traditional vernacular architecture in general — those wonderfully rich idioms created by people all over the world, without the benefit of professional architects! Not only are these indigenous building systems successful in economic, aesthetic and human terms (as any reasonably honest architect will admit), but the socio-economic processes involved in their production are far more appropriate to the situation. For as we have seen earlier, money invested in vernacular housing is pumped into the economy at the *bazaar* level, right where it generates the greatest amount of tertiary employment for those migrants pouring in from the rural areas.

How then does one explain the staggeringly high densities prevailing in Third World cities around the globe? Sadly enough, these generally result not from high-rise buildings, but from an extraordinarily high occupancy rate per room, and by the criminal omission of play spaces, hospitals, schools and other social infrastructure in the neighbourhood. London, for instance, has approximately 3 hectares of green area per thousand people; Delhi has 1.5 hectares; on Bombay island, the figure is 0.1 hectare, and this includes the "grass" on the traffic islands! Even roads, which usually account for at least 25% of land use (higher in Los Angeles!) are only 8% in Bombay island. So naturally the gross residential densities are astronomical, reaching figures which make living conditions quite impossible.

Yet merely increasing the green areas or *maidans* does not solve the problem for they are not used by the entire populace, but only by certain age groups for cricket, football and other such games. No toddler of two or three years would dare to play on them, nor do middle-aged couples use them for evening strolls. On the other hand, the pavements along the seafront in Bombay (which incidentally do not show up in the statistics) are the great community spaces of our city.

Obviously, we should generate many more such promenades. They are the heart of the social life of the tropical temperate zones. In Latin cities such as Paris, Rome and Rio de Janeiro this has always been understood; hence the boulevards with wide pavements and side-walk cafes. Land used for such boulevards is far more cost-effective than conventional "green areas". (Perhaps one tree on the Boulevard San Michel is worth an acre of green in the Bois de Bologne?)

In conclusion it must be emphasised that any investigation of optimal densities is largely determined by the scale of the context we establish. For instance, to a developer looking at an individual

High occupancy per room!

Maidans *are pre-empted by sportsmen* . . .

. . . but the sea front is a promenade for the whole family.

urban site, the trade-off between cost of construction (which rises with building height) and the land component (which varies inversely with the floor space generated), will lead to a certain density. To an authority responsible for a larger context — say an entire neighbourhood — this trade-off will yield a completely different answer, since the area needed for schools, roads, and other infrastructure must be taken into account. To anyone looking at the overall city, in fact at the whole nation and its resources, the answer will change again. Given the awesome scale of urban growth facing the Third World, there can be little doubt that it is within the larger parameters that this issue should be viewed.

For too long we have allowed the densities of our cities to be determined in the narrowest context by the random and self-

Strolling along a Parisian boulevard.

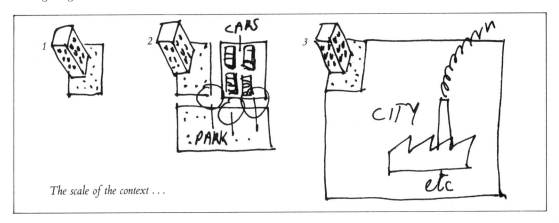

The scale of the context . . .

Piling up the boxes.

interested decisions of individual commercial developers. Higher densities have triggered higher land values in an increasingly vicious spiral, like a serpent feeding off its own tail.

Today, nearly the entire building industry in our major cities turns out a product that only the middle and upper classes can afford, forcing half of our society out on to the pavements. In their confusion and desperation, architects and engineers search for "miracle" technologies, rather like the medieval alchemist's fevered hunt for the touchstone which would convert dross into gold. For too long have we struggled for answers when from the beginning the question has been wrongly formulated in the first place. The problem of housing the vast majority of our urban people is not one of miracle building materials or construction technologies; it is primarily a matter of density, of *re-establishing land-use allocations*.

3

Equity

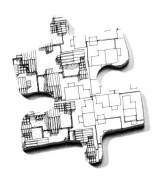

Saana, Yemen.

Over the centuries, every society has produced the housing it needs, naturally and indigenously. Mykonos, Jaiselmet, Saana... these are not habitats "designed" by outsiders, they are the end-products of a process organic to society, like flowers that bloom in a meadow. If adequate housing is not appearing in our cities it is a sign that something is wrong with the system. Our job is to understand the malfunction and try to set it right.

Instead, we immediately start to *design* housing. Why do we do this? Despite apparent good intentions, our attitude is really quite ugly. It seems that we want to believe that the poor do not have houses because of their ignorance; we have to show them how. This is easier on our conscience than the truth: they are homeless because they are on the losing end of the system.

It's an absurd situation . . . as if there were a famine, and in order to feed the great mass of starving millions, architects and housewives ran around writing cookbooks. If people are starving it is not because they don't know how to cook, it is because they do not possess the ingredients!

What magic ingredients make flowers bloom, naturally and spontaneously? One of the most crucial factors is *density*. Beyond a certain level, societal processes break down. This is why, right up to the World War II, Bombay could attract a great number of immigrants without having to throw them destitute on the pavements of the city. Only in recent years have the municipal zoning policies swung away from low-rise buildings in favour of more sophisticated and expensive solutions: the additional cost met by raising the selling price of the units. And with the appalling scarcity of urban land in our cities (because of their obsolete and overloaded structural patterns), it is easy for the developer to command high prices.

Yet by increasing the *supply* of urban land, residential densities can be kept within an optimal range of between 250 to 1000 persons per hectare. Going beyond these densities puts the Third World city into deep trouble. The analogue to body temperature is very tempting: we all know we are ill when we cross 98.6 ° F; perhaps there is a similar indicator for cities? One suspects that this is true not only for the Third World, but for industrialised countries as well. The difference in *overall* densities between London and Paris, for example, is only marginal, but makes a sensational contrast in the kind of accommodation available to the average resident of these two cities. Paris is a marvellous creation, but to live well there you have to be rich. Most citizens make do with a poky little apartment, while in London nearly every family has a terrace house with a garden.

Unfortunately the notion of low-rise housing is associated with the kind of sprawl one sees in the suburbs of western cities, but this, of course, is not what we are talking about. In its concentrated form, low-rise housing is the timeless and classic pattern of residential land-use. It has a number of crucial advantages:

1. It is *incremental.* That is, it can grow with the owner's requirements and his earning capacity. This advantage may soon

Row houses in London.

become a political imperative in Third World countries, where available resources — for the next few years at least — will be pre-empted by other priorities.

2. It has great *variety*, since the individual owner can design and build according to his own needs.

3 This pattern is sensitive to the social/cultural/religious determinants of our environment — factors which are of increasing concern in developing countries. It is relatively easy for the people to adjust the spaces to suit their own preferred *lifestyles*.

4. It makes for *speedier* provision of housing, since an individual building his own house is a highly motivated person. Furthermore, this initiative engenders an increase in per capita savings, so that housing is built without sacrificing other national investment targets.

5. A low-rise building has a much shorter construction period than a high-rise complex. Thus, the *interest cost* of capital tied up during construction is considerably less.

6. High-priority construction materials need not be used. Multistorey buildings must use steel and cement, commodities which are in excruciatingly short supply in developing

Kotachiwadi . . . an old and classic example of low-rise high-density housing in the heart of Bombay.

Housing adapted to local culture.

countries. In contrast, individual houses can be made out of just about anything, starting with bamboo and mud-bricks, then *improved over time*.

7. Admittedly, if the house is constructed of inexpensive materials, then it may not have a life span of more than 15 or 20 years — as compared to a concrete structure with a life span of about 70 years. But this impermanence is really an advantage. For after 20 years, when our economy improves, we will presumably have more resources to devote to housing. As Charles Abrams pointed out, *renewability* should be one of the prime objectives of mass housing in developing countries; for as the nation's economy develops, the housing patterns can change. And this option can be ensured by assigning housing sites not to individual owners themselves but to co-operatives of, say, 20 to 50 families. In time, perhaps 2 or 3 decades from now, the whole parcel of land can be re-developed in keeping with the technological and economic advances of that day. The ugly multi-storey concrete tenement slums built by governmental housing agencies all over the Third World are really the work of pessimists. What they are saying is: we aren't going to have any future.

embrace low-rise

8. Maintenance is much easier on low-rise buildings. The cheapest whitewash can be slapped on by a person on top of an ordinary ladder. In contrast, high-rise buildings are not only expensive to maintain (painting them requires special external scaffolding) but they rise above the tree tops, spoiling the skyline for miles around. This phenomenon is becoming a horrific problem in most Third World cities.

But for the Third World there is one other advantage to this pattern of housing that may prove to be the most decisive of all, and that is *Equity*.

High-rise, high expenses, high maintenance.

Locked into equality.

Today the amount of urban space one controls is directly proportional to one's status and/or income; it has no connection with actual family size. Poor people have families at least as large as rich people; often larger. This space differential, therefore, cannot be justified in human terms, only in economic ones. By contrast consider the cities of Australia where almost every family has a quarter-acre lot — no more, no less. Australia is locked into equality – it can never become elitist. The exact opposite is true of most of the Third World. Despite all our rhetoric about social justic and equal opportunity, we are *locked into inequality*. Our cities make sure of that.

This inequality is directly generated by the grotesque skew of the income profile, yet the pattern of high-density low-rise housing gives us a way out of the dilemma. Plot sizes ranging from 50 square metres to 100 square metres can be viable both for the poorest sections of society (furnished perhaps with just a couple of trees, a tied-up goat, and a lean-to roof) as well as for the affluent. Consider, for example, the elegant town-houses of Amsterdam, San Francisco, and Udaipur. In fact, these optimally-sized plots — we can call them *Equity Plots* — could be viable for more than 95 percent of our urban population. This is indeed a concept with profound socio-political implications; one which could constitute a crucial step towards defining a truly egalitarian urban society, totally different from that now prevailing in most Third World cities.

A policy of Equity Plots has the added advantage of not pre-determining the social and economic mix either in neighbourhoods or across the city. Most planning today, no matter how liberal the intention, ends up with a rigid caste system of residential areas. Chandigarh is a good example. The reason for this is simple. Since the plots are of vastly different sizes, planners have to decide *beforehand* about their positioning within a sector. In such a situation, a planner cannot place clerks' houses cheek-by-jowl with those of Ministers, and once the plan has been implemented on site, the pattern cannot be changed. So we get cities which are rigid and inflexible. They cannot respond to the social forces constantly at work which make older "un-designed" cities such an organic mix of income groups and communities.

If there ever is a bill of rights for housing in the Third World, it will surely have to include — enshrine! — the cardinal principles:

Incrementality	**Equity**
Pluralism	**Open-to-sky space**
Participation	**Disaggregation**
Income generation	

The same size plot can work for a rich family . . .

. . . or a poor one.

54

What these principles predicate are patterns in which units are packed close enough to provide the advantages of high density, yet separate enough to allow for individual identity and growth.

This can be seen in a housing sector of Belapur, a node just adjacent to the city centre of New Bombay: The site measures about 5.5 hectares. On the basis of the opportunity cost of the land, the planning brief specified a density of 500 persons or 100 households per hectare. In addition, the accommodation had to cover almost the entire range of income groups, from the lowest, (with a budget of Rs. 20,000 per dwelling unit), to the upper-middle categories (with a budget of Rs. 180,000).

To ensure that the dwelling units will all be incremental, each is placed on its own individual site. The main walls supporting the roof or the upper floors are not shared in common with any neighbour. This independence not only minimises the amount of collaboration — and quarrels! — involved in essential undertakings such as roof repairs, but also allows each of the houses to be extended unilaterally.

Although the range of income groups is large (a ratio of 1:5), the variation in plot size is quite small, from 45 square metres to 75 square metres (a ratio of much less than 1:2). Originally one standard Equity Plot of 50 square metres for all income groups was planned, but this had to be amended slightly because of rules and procedures specified by the lending agencies.

Housing at Belapur, designed by the author.

Income Group (Rupees per Month)	Percentage of Households	Cumulative Percentage
UP TO 325	7	7
326–650	16	23
651–900	17	40
901–1100	14	54
1101–1600	20	74
1601–2500	16	90
2500 +	10	100

Poverty line (between 651–900 and 901–1100 rows)

The physical plan is based on the open/enclosed space trade-off discussed earlier. Within the plot, each family has open-to-sky space (kitchen yards, terraces, etc.) to augment the built-up area. The circulation and community areas are arranged in a pattern which sets up the hierarchy of spaces discussed in Chapter 2.

Usually, low-rise high-density housing takes the form of row-houses, organised along monotonous linear corridors.

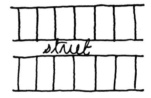

In this case, the units are clustered instead around small community spaces. At the smallest scale, 7 units are grouped around an intimate courtyard 8 metres × 8 metres.

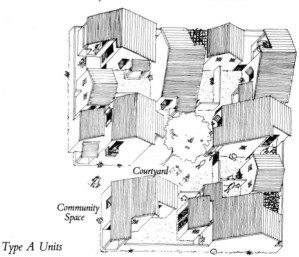

Courtyard

Community Space

Type A Units

Three of these clusters combine to form a bigger module of 21 houses, surrounding an open space 12 metres × 12 metres.

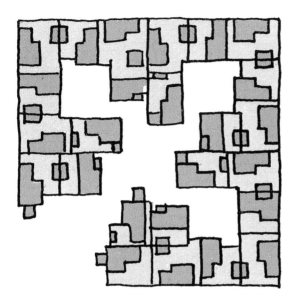

Three such modules interlock to define the next scale of community space — approximately 20 metres × 20 metres.

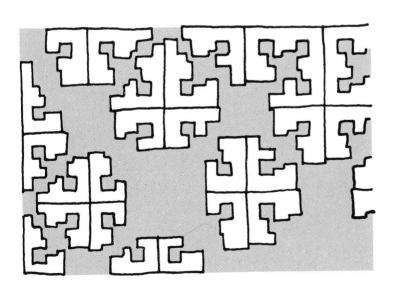

This spatial hierarchy continues until one reaches the largest neighbourhood spaces where primary schools and other similar facilities are located. Down the centre runs a small stream which drains off surface water during the monsoons.

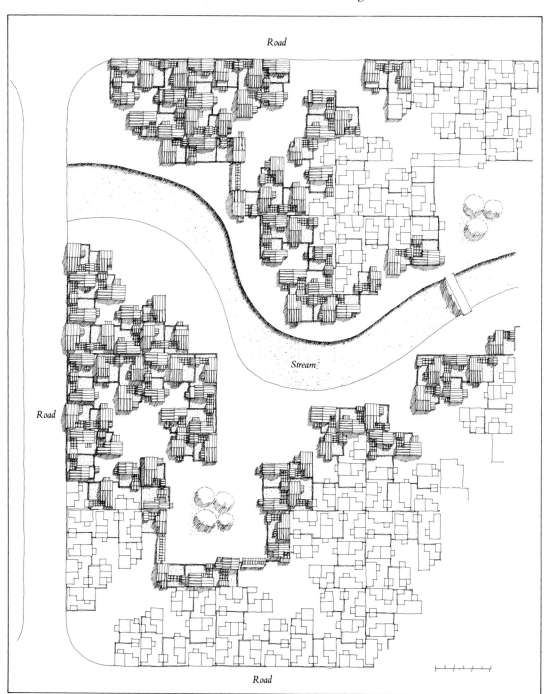

The typology of the houses forms two sets. Within each set, the houses can grow incrementally to the next state of development, as family income increases.

Typology of houses

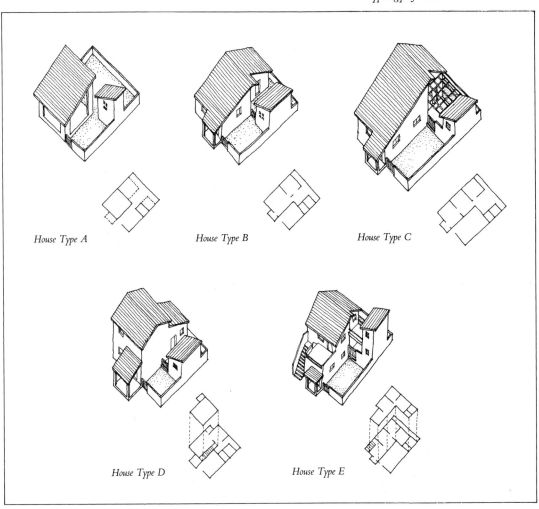

House Type A

House Type B

House Type C

House Type D

House Type E

Section: Type B

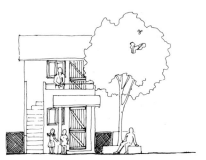

Elevation: Type C

In Belapur, the house sites are arranged with the toilets located in pairs to save on plumbing and sanitation costs. For each site, the main structure of the house can abut the boundary on two clearly specified edges — in a pattern which ensures that it will be free-standing with respect to its neighbours. No windows are allowed in these walls, so as to protect the privacy of all concerned.

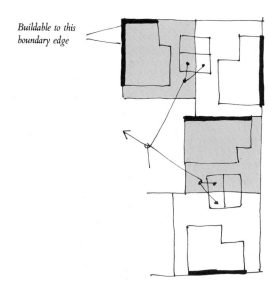

Buildable to this boundary edge

A hierarchy of spaces.

Personalising one's habitat.

These house plans and drawings are merely indicative. Construction of the units is simple enough to be undertaken by local masons and *mistris*, with the active participation of the people themselves. In time, the occupants will add their own overlays of colour and symbols, colonising it with their lifestyles.

Housing at Belapur, New Bombay.

4

Mobility

Getting to work in China.

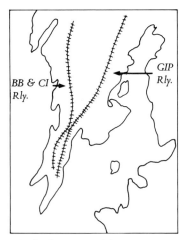

The chief engineers of the two railway lines (GIP and BB & CI) were the real planners of Bombay.

Probably one of the most vivid images of urban China is of a wide avenue of trees, filled with people in blue clothes all cycling to work. It is a happy, positive image, one which underlines the primary importance of the bicycle in developing countries. For a low capital investment, the bicycle provides an individual mobility with no concomitant costs for petrol or other fuel. Bicycles are energy-sane and pollution-free.

The landscape of our Third World city should certainly include special bicycle paths, so that they are protected from automobiles and in turn do not interfere with the pedestrians. Where already available, these paths have proven very popular; but even in cities where they do not exist, people cycle great distances to work — so fundamental is the bicycle as a mode of transport in the Third World.

Yet obviously, as the city gets larger, this viability decreases, both because of the distances involved, and because of the increased density of cross-city traffic clogging the main arteries. Some sort of public transport then becomes advantageous.

Now a public transport system is, almost by definition, a linear function. It is viable only in the context of a land-use plan which develops corridors of high density demand. Bombay, for

Victoria Terminus, Bombay: half a million people arriving every morning . . . nobody leaving.

instance, is a linear city based on two parallel commuter train corridors. Even today, for a few rupees one can buy a month-long railway pass valid for an unlimited number of journeys from north to south — a distance of over 40 kilometres. New Delhi, on the other hand, being a low-density sprawl of even distribution, cannot support an economical mass transport system.

In fact in the evenly-spread mesh of a city like New Delhi, it is best to be individually mobile (whether by car or jet-propelled roller skates), since a traffic jam encountered at one intersection can always be bypassed with a detour to another point on the grid. This is why the decision-makers of India, almost all of whom travel in private cars, think Delhi is the "better" of the two cities. For the average citizen quite the reverse is actually the case, and the difference between the services provided by the bus company in Bombay and that in Delhi is not merely one of management — it is inherent in the physical layout of the two cities themselves.

To attempt a viable mass transport system in Delhi will necessitate first creating a series of linear sub-structures. That is to say, into the existing land-use pattern we must in-lay high-density housing developments in a manner which generates corridors of demand, down which the mass transport will run. At each transit stop along these corridors there will then exist a hinterland of sufficient density to support a public transport system. Assuming that an acceptable walking distance to the mass rapid transit (MRT) station to be about 8 minutes, establishes a hinterland of about 50 hectares on each side of the station. We have already seen how, giving each family a small individual plot, a density of 500 people per hectare can be achieved. This comes to 25,000 persons living on each side of the station, i.e. about 50,000 per transit stop, which

*The spread of New Delhi defies
efficient public transport.*

is more than enough to support an economical rapid mass transit system.

By locating employment centres *within* housing areas, travel distances and costs can be further reduced and sometimes even eliminated altogether. In this respect, the age-old patterns of work-dwelling mix found all over the Third World (as in the shop-houses of South-East Asia) are far more humane and economical than the exclusive zonal systems introduced by modern town planning.

Different transport systems (from bicyle to bus to train) operate under different cost/capacity constraints. This suggests a hierarchy of transport systems implemented in succession as the city grows. Thus, starting with bicycles and buses in mixed traffic, we can gradually build to more heavy-duty systems, without transgressing at any stage the cost/capacity constraints we face.

There is another important advantage in this approach: a single mass transport system generates what is essentially a linear corridor, which usually imposes a severe constraint on site planning. By

Shop houses in Bombay: A direct relationship of work and residence which not only avoids commuting but is simple enough to encourage family businesses — which means more economic activity in the bazaar sector, just where the jobs are most needed.

Bombay: Morning rush hour.

combining 2 or 3 compatible transport systems, the plan is freed from the constraint of a narrow ribbon development and considerable physical planning advantages can accrue. Furthermore, and of prime importance, the interchanges between systems will constitute natural nodal points in the city's growth.

Here, for instance, is a series of sectors (mixed residential and work) along a bus line, with each bus stop constituting a natural point of growth. Such a linear system makes for a corridor of medium-density demand, and thus for an efficient bus system.

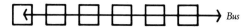

Here are the same sectors, but now arranged on a grid, (as, for instance, in Chandigarh). In such a pattern, the bus service is far less economical than in the linear pattern shown above, and the citizens need to be individually mobile.

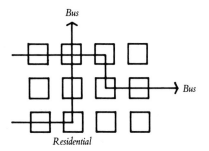

However, our linear pattern can also, with time, prove to be a disadvantage, for as population density intensifies, traffic grows and clogs the artery. A primary MRT then becomes necessary. To install a train track down the centre of development would involve either acquiring developed land, and knocking down buildings or reserving this land at the start — which is difficult, both because of squatters, and because to do so would, for the first several years, leave a scar of no-man's land running down the middle of the sectors.

Keeping the train alignment outside the system is a better alternative. The train stations — less numerous than the bus stops — occur only once every 4th or 5th sector, with the train track itself kept outside the intermediate sectors. However, this results in a somewhat devious and illogical train alignment.

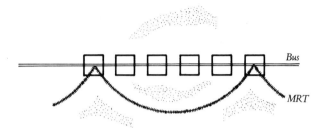

Why not reverse the pattern? Start with a bus line which meanders; later on, when the train is installed, its alignment is direct. This pattern more clearly reflects the alignment constraints of the two systems.

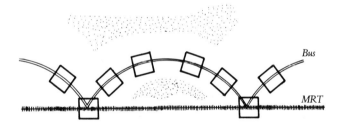

How the system grows. We start with a bus line (secondary MRT) generating a series of sectors of approximately equal importance. Let's call them type A. Perhaps one, because of its particular location (near the water?), grows in importance. Let's call it type B.

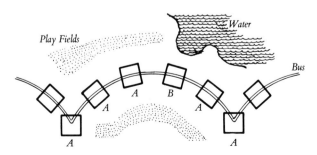

As the traffic grows and the primary MRT is installed, the interchanges generate additional activity, upgrading these particular sectors — type C.

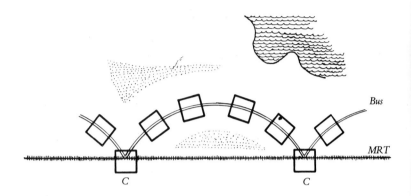

With time, a secondary bus line can be installed opening up a whole new section of the hinterland.

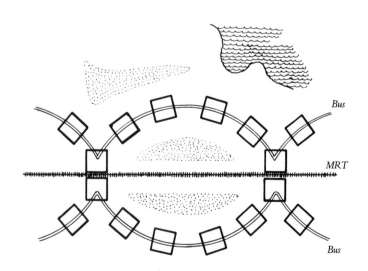

The diagram below shows the proposed system on a typical portion of the New Bombay site, which runs between hills and water.

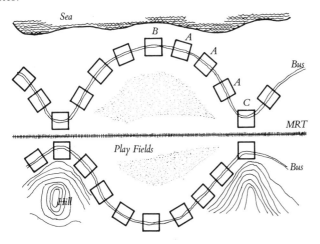

In future, should densities and traffic grow beyond expectation, an additional primary MRT can be installed. This will upgrade the importance of some type-A sectors, which now provide an opportunity to locate new social infrastructure and other facilities for the growing population. Human settlements have always tended to locate at transport junctions, on a scale directly proportional to the importance of the junction. At the major nodal points, higher densities can be allowed to develop for specialised functions, such as offices, shopping and luxury apartments. Thus a natural hierarchy of nodal points can develop, culminating in the city centre.

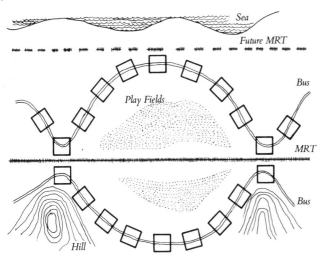

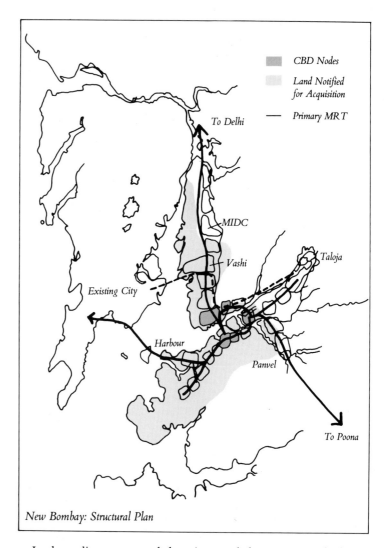

New Bombay: Structural Plan

In these diagrams, work locations and the MRT are deployed to open up urban land, keeping densities in the residential areas at near-optimum levels and thus avoiding the kind of escalating pressures which distort — and finally destroy — our cities. Even if a subsidy for the MRT is required, it is, in effect, an *indirect subsidy on housing* — more economical and effective than *direct* housing subsidies which lead, only too often, to illegal transfer of the dwelling units. The point is important. Giving the squatter a dwelling unit at a price much lower than its market value merely tempts him to sell it for profit — and move back onto the pavements (as has happened time and again all over the Third World). A subsidy on public transport, on the other hand, opens up even more housing, without either the temptation or the opportunity for resale.

Because of the scale of urban growth expected in the Third World, it will be impossible to enforce a fixed and pre-conceived end picture. Rather, open-ended planning is called for: not a 'frozen' master plan, but the setting forth of a series of growth options, a flexible structural plan which indicates potential growth points.

Historically these have usually been points of intersection and/or transfer. For instance, the junction of two roads is usually a good place to locate a cigarette stall. So also a bus stop, where people transfer from one mode of travel (walking) to another (vehicular). Even a great seaport like Bombay is just that: a point of transfer from land to sea. This function has been the dynamo generating its growth.

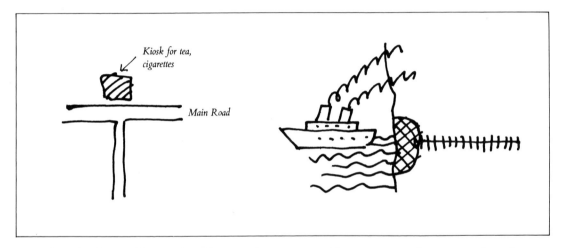

Points of intersection and transfer.

In the Third World, we should try, wherever possible, to illustrate our planning proposals not with imaginary perspectives, but with actual photographs of real-life conditions, representing successive snapshots of the growth process we are proposing. Only then can we ensure that we are involving the organic — truly *biological* — nature of urban growth.

Transport is not an entity in itself. It is part of an intricate feed-back mechanism involving other locational decisions of the city. Too often, traffic engineers are given a brief where the existing land-use pattern is an unquestionable "given"; then they have to postulate a traffic "solution'. So they usually come up with an expensive system of freeways, tunnels, flyovers, and so forth. Yet we know that such palliatives are short-lived; ease of movement encourages more journeys, thus clogging the arteries once again. *Journeys always multiply to the point of clogging* — it is a kind of Parkinson's Law in transport planning!

Land-use and transport patterns are but two sides of the same coin. By modifying land-use patterns, we might be able to drasti-

Transportation is only one side of the coin.

cally *alter* desire lines (and hence traffic flow) at a mere fraction of the usual cost. Land-use, desire lines, transport systems and the opportunity cost of land are all inextricably interconnected. Properly understood and manipulated, they can provide planning authorities with the tools necessary to deal with the urban growth ahead.

This line of thinking is more relevant to Third World cities than to those in the West where urban population have already stabilised and planners feel that only a certain amount of "fine-tuning" is called for. Thus many of the techniques of Western planning are irrelevant to the Third World, where problems are almost diametrically opposite. New York is trying to woo people back to the city; Shanghai or Bogota or Hong Kong are trying to keep them out. Planners in the Third World will have to develop their own techniques — if necessary from scratch — if they are to be effective.

5

Great City...
Terrible Place

Man does not live by bread alone . . .
The Pampalona bull races.

Perhaps we are paying too much attention to the physical and economic aspects of a city and not enough to its mythical, its metaphysical, attributes. For a city can be beautiful as physical habitat — with trees, uncrowded roads, open spaces — and yet fail to provide that particular, ineffable quality of urbanity which we call "city".

We all know examples of this. Bombay, of course, illustrates the very opposite. Every day it gets worse and worse as physical environment . . . and yet better and better as "city". That is to say, everyday, on every level of society — from squatter to college student to entrepreneur to artist — it offers more in the way of skills, activities and opportunities.

The vitality of the theatre with its ever-growing audiences; the range and variety of newspapers and magazines; a hundred indications emphasise that impaction (implosion!) of energy and people which really is a two-edged sword . . . destroying Bombay as environment, while intensifying its quality as city.

Teilhard de Chardin likened this increasing complexity (which we also experience as we move from village to town to city) with the successive folding of a handkerchief on itself: each fold doubles the layers of material, the density of experience. As a biologist, he

felt the move towards complexity is as compulsive and as irreversible as the blind drive that caused life to develop from single-cells to more and more complex forms. It is an intriguing insight, and perhaps explains not only why the migrant goes from village to town, but, more importantly, why, having experienced the physical degradation of his new life, he does not return to his village. He has no choice. We only go back to Walden Pond when we can take our complexity with us. Only the madman or the mystic goes out into the desert. And the mystic is really taking his God, his complexity, with him. That leaves only the madman.

Ganpathi festival at Chowpatty beach, Bombay.

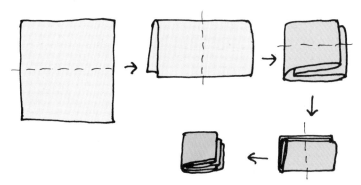

Increasing complexity.

An equally incisive explanation of the lure of cities was put forward by the Greek planner Doxiadis, the founder of Ekistics. I remember a slide-show he gave, many years ago ... 60 millimetre slides throwing huge clear, monumental images on the screen ... First slide: a diagram of a village: 250 red dots and 1 blue one — he's a blue person. Einstein? The village idiot? Anyway, he's different from the rest.

Next slide: a town of 1000 people. Now there are 4 or 5 blue dots floating around.

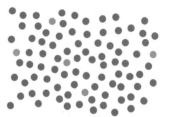

Next: a town of 25,000 people. Ah! A historic moment: 2 blue people are meeting for the first time.

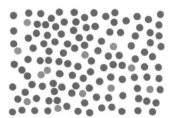

Now a town of 100,000 ... and several colonies where blue people reside. Furthermore, some of the red dots on the fringes of these colonies are turning ... purple!

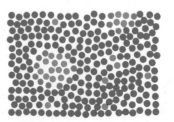

That's what cities are about. Blue people getting together. Communicating. Reinforcing each other. Challenging (and changing!) the red ones. Like the Quit India Movement announced by Mahatma Gandhi from a *maidan* in Bombay. And Calcutta, during its heyday in the twenties, a powerhouse of political, religious and artistic ideas and reforms. Hence also the paradox: Bombay *decaying* as a physical plant, yet *improving* as a city — as a place where different people meet, where things happen, where ideas incubate.

And also, of course, as a place where urban skills grow. For the developing world needs these skills. Today in the Arabian Gulf, a surprisingly large proportion of development is in the hands of Third World technocrats: engineers, doctors, nurses, construction firms, hoteliers. They are winning contracts in the face of worldwide competition, from clients who have a global choice. It is truly an extraordinary achievement — and primarily for our urban centres which produce these skills.

Gandhiji launching the "Quit India" movement in Bombay, 1942.

Indian nurses in the Gulf: urban skills.

Parisians discussing their monarch.

Development necessitates management, and too often the Third World has to import managerial know-how (via the World Bank and the United Nations). Fortunately India has a wide spectrum of urban centres, varying from small market towns to the great metropolii, producing an incredible range and diversity of skills. Like the farmlands of the Punjab or the coalfields of Bihar, they are a *crucial* part of our national wealth. To let the cities deteriorate is to squander priceless resources — a blunder of the highest order.

Our criminal indifference to cities like Calcutta or Bombay over the last decades have allowed conditions to deteriorate to sub-human levels. Yet somehow Bombay functions, and with an energy and enthusiasm that is far more impressive than a show-piece capital like Delhi, because the budget available there per

Energy and enthusiasm, Multan, Pakistan.

capita is several-fold that of Bombay. Furthermore, cities like Bombay and Calcutta represents a true cross-section of urban incomes, whereas New Delhi has no destitute people (they are all hidden in Old Delhi); the poorest people one sees are government clerks cycling to work, and in winter even they are dressed in woolens! The Third World has too many examples of such capital cities, cities whose apparent affluence is misleading — most of all to the politicians and bureaucrats who live there.

No, the miracle of Bombay is that despite political indifference and apathy, despite lack of resources, some water does get distributed (at least most of the time), buses and trains provide public transport all day and most of the night, etc ... all accomplished by the skill, energy and dedication of the people of this city. Yet how long can this last? How long before the neglect, the piles of debris, the stinking garbage take their toll — and the elan, the enthusiasm, of the citizens slowly disintegrates? Then, as in the case of Calcutta, a kind of apathy begins to set in, a stultifying indifference.

Cities have always been *unique* indicators of civilisation — from Mohenjodaro to Athens, from Persepolis to Isfahan, from Beijing to Rome. Great music can be created during rotten times, even painting, and poetry, but never great architecture and cities. Why is this so? Primarily because building involves two essential conditions: firstly an economic system which concentrates power and decision-making; and secondly, at the centre of that decision-making, leaders with the vision, the taste and the political will to deploy these resources intelligently.

Fatehpur-Sikri: one of the greatest indicators of civilisation.

81

The first set of conditions prevails only too often; the second hardly ever. The combination is almost unique. Thus Akbar will always be Akbar. Not because of his military exploits — those have been bettered a hundred times, both before and after his time. He will always be Akbar because, at the centre of that vortex of power, he exercised these qualities.

Cities grow . . . and die . . . much faster than we think. Visiting Calcutta today, it is difficult to understand how turn-of-the-century travellers could have deemed it as one of the great metropolii of the world — the finest East of Suez, a "jewel in the crown". Could they not see the grave, perhaps terminal, illness already tightening its grip on that marvellously humane city? No,

Calcutta in the 1880s . . .

. . . and a hundred years later.

82

obviously there is a time lag during which calamity is not overt. So that even late into the 1940s and 1950s we still could not see the fatal symptoms ... the writing on the wall.

The same is true of Bombay. While it is getting better and better as city, and disintegrating — rapidly and quite unnecessarily — as environment, perhaps what we are experiencing is the last burst of energy, the spastic twitches before the end. Living in this city we wouldn't notice it ourselves.

The city environment: gradually boiling to death in a state of euphoria.

If a frog is dropped into a saucepan of very hot water, it will desperately try to hop out. But place a frog in tepid water and then very very gradually raise the temperature ... the frog will swim around happily ... adjusting to the increasingly dangerous conditions. In fact, just before the end, just before the frog begins to cook ... when the water is exceedingly hot ... the frog relaxes and a state of euphoria sets in (as in hot-tub baths). Maybe that is happening to us in Bombay, as every day we find it to be more and more a *great city* ... and a *terrible* place.

But perhaps this has always been true of all the world's great metropolii. We are so immersed in their mythical qualities we do not see their physical reality. If you were to visit Manhattan but could not feel or comprehend its myths, what would you see? A monotonous grid of traffic intersections and buildings like pigeon-holes, much like Cleveland, Detroit and a dozen other North American cities. But Fifth Avenue ... Central Park ... 42nd Street ... the very names are magic! We do not hear them for what they really are — mere numbers on a map, planners' shorthand. They are the stuff dreams are made of!

So also with the burgeoning metropolii of the Third World. What to the outsider may appear a mere mass of humanity spreading in all directions to infinity, to the people themselves could well be a place of unique opportunity with truly mythical dimensions.

A grid of pidgeon-holes . . .

. . . but ah, Manhattan!

6

Disaggregating
the Numbers

The power and the glory ... of Big Arithmetic!

The numbers we have been discussing are astronomical, beyond human comprehension — which poses a danger, of course. We can get high on this arithmetic, as some of the British Viceroys did when they thought of all the natives in need of "civilisation", and the Victorian missionaries when they contemplated the billions of Asian and African souls waiting to be "saved".

To avoid this very real danger, it is essential that we disaggregate the numbers. Only then can we begin to see them clearly. If we consider, for example, the remarkable opus of Modern Architecture in this century, we find that the most glaring failure has been in the field of mass housing. Without doubt, the architects earnestly and sincerely believed they were creating a humane and liveable habitat. In actual fact, in most cases what they produced was faceless, ugly, and dull. Was this a failure of designer talent? I think not. Rather, it was an inevitable outcome of *methodology*, of the way we picked up the problem.

The enormous success of Henry Ford's assembly line and similar 20th-century miracles seduced architects into thinking that the analogue of the mass-produced car was appropriate in the field of housing. Even Le Corbusier — or *especially* Le Corbusier — fell for this analogy with his Citrohan housing. The principle involved

Workers' housing by Walter Gropius.

Cloning suburban houses . . .

. . . and high-rise towers.

was apparently this: first to create the *ideal* house and then *clone* it. Unfortunately, in practice, it does not work. For without doubt:

Ideal House x 10,000 ≠ Ideal Community

Henry Ford's methods did not take into account many of the things we find are essential to housing: variety, identity, participation — in short, *pluralism*. Louis Mumford was intuitively right when he criticised modern architects for trying to identify an ideal set of environmental conditions: such and such degree temperature, so much percent humidity, and so forth. The search, Mumford pointed out, was doomed to failure, since ideal conditions were, by definition, *varying* conditions. Given human nature, it is impossible to establish a fixed static condition as the perfect one. Our way of perceiving the task was wrong, and doomed to failure.

One fears that much the same error continues even today in housing. The first step (into the trap) is to aggregate demand. This usually includes not only current demand but also backlog, and often future demand as well. The numbers arrived at are colossal — and start the architect's adrenalin flowing!

The next fatal step — and the one which springs the trap — is to set up large centralised agencies to deal with this aggregated demand. No matter whether the centralised agency is governmental or organised by private developers, the resulting method is the same: *count their legs and divide by four*.

Very often, the faceless inhuman results are mistakenly believed to be the outcome of a particular political ideology, but of course politics has nothing to do with it. Such housing is found all over

Prisoners of the process: in the U.S.A. . . .

. . . and in the U.S.S.R.

the world; in the Bronx, in Moscow, in Singapore, in Bombay, at the Portes of Paris. *It is the direct result of the process.* For with the aggregated numbers comes the temptation to clone. In other words, having to house 10,000 families, the architect designs a building which can accommodate say, 500 of them, which means that 20 such buildings will have to be built. And that's it: Q.E.D. The bureaucrat in the large centralised agency for whom the architect works loves this solution; it makes for a very clean office file! He can, for any given financial year, make precise estimates of exactly how much cement and brick and steel he will need, and he can present a well-organised budget to his political bosses. No wonder he is happy. It is the exact opposite of the pluralistic, dis-aggregated, messy, user-participation processes we have been discussing.

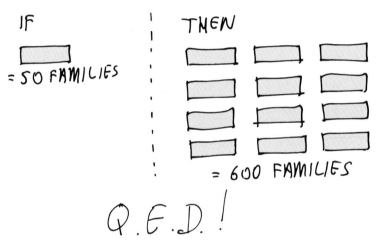

IF

= 50 FAMILIES

THEN

= 600 FAMILIES

Q.E.D.!

Modern architects in the 1920s were the first to walk into the trap — this was in the aftermath of World War I and was probably the first time that Europeans became aware of such large numbers. The effect was mind-blowing. It triggered off a great burst of feverish building. The next time was in the years immediately following World War II. Again there was a frenzied response, most of it disastrous! Now the danger has moved to the Third World, for it is here that the big numbers are surfacing. Colossal aggregates completely dwarfing anything thrown up by Europe. Are we going to repeat the same mistakes?

If not, we must *change the process.* An analogy to food may be useful here: For instance, on any given evening, there is a need for 6 million dinners in Paris. That's the first step: we've aggregated the demand. Now, the next. Staggered by the size of the figure, we hurriedly calculate that the most efficient way to deal with the problem will be to set up 50 central kitchens, each producing

Corbusier's hand. Creating life — or destroying it?

Contentment in the kitchen . . . serving the Parisian population.

120,000 dinners. Perhaps the dinners will all be produced by the end of the day, but will they be edible?

Fortunately for the French, no such thing is happening to food production in Paris. No one aggregates the demand, and the 6 million dinners get quietly cooked in the hundreds of thousands of kitchens across the city. We need an analagous methodology for producing housing. It would take a highly inventive management to design it, but it *must* come into being. It is a crucial pre-requisite of the new landscape.

As Hassan Fathy, the great Egyptian architect, once said: "Nobody should design more than 12 houses at a time. If you take the greatest surgeon in the world and ask him to operate on 200 people in a day — he'll kill them all!"

7

Political Will

Third World paradigm.

There is a syndrome common to most Third World urban centres. Each seems to consist of two different cities, one is for the poor, another (interlocked with it) for the rich. Very often the latter has a special name. In Bombay, for instance, it is called "The Fort". In Dakar, Senegal, it is "The Plateau" — an astonishingly accurate name, both in terms of geography, as well as the economic/psychological realities of that city.

Although these two worlds occupy quite separate territories, rich and poor enjoy a symbiotic relationship. This relationship is not always understood by the rich, who often overlook the fact that they need the poor to run the city — not to mention their own households. In most of Bombay's privileged homes, a multitude of tasks, from the daily washing of the car to the weekly laundry, are regularly performed — for a pittance — by squatters. Ironically, if the squatters in Bombay had to pay for regular accommodation, the cost of their services would rise beyond what their employers could afford! (They are an analogue of the "guest workers" of Europe and the Mexican "wetbacks" in Texas.)

In order to decrease this disparity of income and move towards a more equitable society, some Third World governments have tried to reduce the holdings of the rich by socialising the land. For instance, some years ago, the Government of India passed an act which places a ceiling on owning urban property. Any surplus land has to be surrendered to the Government, at a minimal price, for construction of low-income housing.

Unfortunately this law has not been effective, because the surplus land exists in little fragments all over the city — and often (because of lack of access to jobs, mass transport, etc.) in locations quite unsuitable for low-income housing. What is needed is not an acquisition act which nets haphazard little parcels of real estate, but one which delivers large chunks of land at a *scale*, and in *locations* which would allow our cities to undertake the re-structuring they so desperately need. In that sense, the act is radical enough to galvanise the rich into a defensive action (which has effectively frozen almost all land transactions in our urban centres and thus, ironically, sent the value of the existing buildings even

The two faces of Bombay: the gleaming metropolis . . .

. . . and the squalor.

higher!). At the same time, it is not draconian enough to precipitate any real change in the pattern of our cities.

This is indeed a pity. In too many Third World cities, owning land is a prerogative of only a small fraction of the urban elite — and they see this land as an economic commodity that appreciates faster than most other investments. Expropriating land for low-income housing does not always work, since the disparity between the sub-sidised price and the actual market value is considerable and tempts the poor to illegally sell their dwelling units and move back on to the pavements. For expropriation merely removes the market value of the commodity; it does not change the *opportunity cost* of land – which reflects the pressure points in the city, and which in turn are determined by the city's functional structure (transport lines, job locations, etc.). Abolishing private ownership of land in London will not allow everyone to live around Hyde Park. To achieve that goal, London will have to be restructured so as to create more Hyde Parks.

The desire to possess land is evidently a very tenacious one. In New Bombay, despite statutory powers of acquisition, there was enormous resistance from the local farmers and villagers to part with their land — even though it was only of marginal yield. They were not against the idea of the new city; they just wanted to hold on to the land and make the 'profits' themselves. (In fact, they probably wouldn't have got any real profits, having sold out to Bombay developers much too early for that.) Still, it is easy to understand their resentment. After generations of poverty, they thought they finally have a miraculous change of fortune. The result is that even today, land keeps coming in bits and pieces and the development programme has to be constantly readjusted.

Given the crucial objectives of New Bombay, it was tragic indeed that the government tripped up on the very first step: land acquisition. Instead of being generous to the farmers, the bureau-

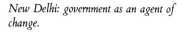

New Delhi: government as an agent of change.

crats always offered too little, too late. Perhaps instead of expropriating the land, the government should have found a way to
allow the owners to exchange their land for equity in the development corporation. New legal structures must be innovated,
structures which motivate human beings to cooperate.

In this connection, it is illuminating to perceive how little of
Bombay was actually *built* by the British — most hospitals,
schools, etc. were commissioned by Indians. What the British did
provide was the civic structure within which the energy and
enthusiasm of the Indians could flourish. That Victorian civic
structure was extremely well suited to the paternalistic caste-bound
Indian society of that time. Today one reason for Bombay's break-
down is that its civic structure does not relate to the new social
realities of the city, does not in any way involve or motivate the
4 million have-nots who live in illegal squatter settlements. Top
priority: to invent a new civic structure for this city.

Another crucial issue: employment generation — the key to all
urban growth. To take the pressure off Bombay, it is essential that
New Bombay attracts the offices that otherwise proliferate at the
southern tip of the island. But an office cannot start on its own in
the middle of nowhere. There is a certain bundle of inter-related
jobs, a critical mass, which has to be attained before the take-off
point is reached.

A number of studies were undertaken to identify precisely the
critical mass involved, and to determine just *who* could act as the
lead sector. In our original proposals, we suggested that this could
be achieved at one stroke by the State Government moving the
capital function across to the new centre, since it was sure to pull
private business in its wake. The suggestion was not implemented.

For how do you get the decision-makers — the government
ministers, the bureaucrats, the industrialists, the businessmen — to
start a new centre, when they can afford to compete for space in
the old one? Because for the privileged, Bombay is quite a pleasant
city to live in. Schools, clubs, colleges, sports stadia, cinemas,
housing and offices (The Plateau!) are all within a stone's throw
of one another at the southern end of the city.

The facts of the matter are brutally simple. The people who can
pull the levers to change Bombay don't need to change Bombay.
In fact they often stand to gain by the *status quo*. Thus all through
the 70s, simultaneously with developing New Bombay, the State
Government was reclaiming land at Cuffe Parade/Nariman Point,
next to the existing city centre, and selling it for astronomical sums,
creating considerable prosperity for a select few in the process. The
resulting high-rise jungle has enormously increased the strain on
city services such as water supply, public transport and garbage
collection. Finally, by taking the issue directly to the public

95

Malabar Hill

Victona Terminus

Universtiy

Gymkhanas

THE FORT

Museums

Hotels

through citizens' groups, a stop was put to this reclamation. But the compilation of the critical mass of offices needed for New Bombay received a severe setback. We lost at least five years.

Only recently has the momentum begun to build again. Some key wholesale markets (e.g. iron and steel, onions and potatoes) have been moved to New Bombay. There have been massive investments in the new port (which will handle a larger tonnage than the existing docks in Bombay), and in the terminal facilities for oil and natural gas from the off-shore walls at Bombay High. The State Government has moved some of its offices — albeit rather minor ones — around which a commercial node is growing. Today a great deal of construction is in progress, and soon New Bombay's population is expected to exceed 500,000. It has even — and, to me, this is like signs of Spring — begun attracting its own squatters.

Recently there has been pressure to change the policy and allow private ownership of land. Ironically, this would probably increase the pace of New Bombay's growth. In fact, one would not be surprised if, given the political clout of some of Bombay's developers, the Government would then decide to move! However, such a strategy, would not produce housing for the poor. For given the desperately low income levels of the majority of citizens, investing in housing construction in our cities begins to be profitable only at the level of the top 20% of the population, which is why there is such an excessive amount of speculative high-income housing being built — and lying luxuriously vacant — in Bombay, as in most other Third World cities.

The urge to establish territorial rights and build one's own house seems to be primordial and operates at all income levels.

Certainly, as soon as land tenure is assured, the squatter's motivation to improve his habitat grows by leaps and bounds. By the same token, one should not assume that all the housing built by the middle and upper income groups is speculative and antisocial.

Reclaiming land and exploiting the city: Cuffe Parade/Nariman Point.

Building one's own environment.

Much of it is the legitimate and heart-felt concern of the house-holder for the future of his family. This concern can be mobilised for the development of new areas. For while moving to a new growth centre might have little attraction to decision-makers collectively deciding for a business corporation or government department, it could constitute an irresistible advantage to each one of them — and to all the staff — in the context of their own lives.

In a country like India, most working people, from chairman to peon, including of course government officials, worry about that terrifying day (58 years old!) of "retirement", when everything — salary, position, car, house — is taken from them in one fell blow. It's a day to be feared. So most spend the last few years in power feathering their nests, getting a company or government flat permanently allotted to them, and so forth. It is easy to ridicule this activity, and even to condemn it, but it is the outcome of legitimate human concerns.

Now examine another factor in the urban equation; the staggering cost of office and residential space in the heart of our metropolitan cities. Today, because of the disastrous mismatch of demand and supply in Bombay, this market price is more than 8 times the replacement cost of equivalent space in New Bombay. Thus every square metre of office sold in the existing city could not only finance equivalent office space in the new one, but also pay for the housing and social institutions needed for executives and staff. Furthermore, if that housing were given to a worker on retirement (against a deduction of monthly percentage of salary) one of the greatest insecurities of his life would be dispelled. Far from resenting the move to a new context, he might in fact welcome it. After all, the essential principle of all new settlements

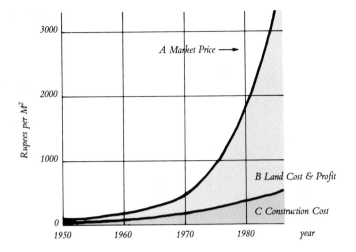

C *rises gradually with inflation.*
A *escalates sharply with the scarcity value of the commodity.* B *expands to mop up the difference. The bigger the gap between* A *and* C, *the better this Decanter Theory works.*

is this: no one minds being a pioneer so long as he gets the rewards that go with it.

Of course such a scheme cannot be open-ended. It is not a long-term strategy, but merely a tactic to start the new pot cooking. It should be announced with a sharp cut-off point; 6 months or the first 50,000 office jobs or whatever critical mass it takes to get the new centre going. The offer should be open to any office establishment, including governmental ones. *Especially* government, so that state employees will be motivated to force (perhaps through a strike?!) the kind of structural changes their ministers are too myopic, or timid, or lazy to make.

Siphoning off existing activity to new areas necessitates an understanding of what might be termed Decanter Theory. Let us imagine Bombay and New Bombay as two beakers — OB and NB — one full, the other quite empty. If we could siphon off some of the contents of OB, we would like them to be replaced by open spaces and social infrastructure. Yet this is hardly likely to happen. The city does not have the financial resources to buy the existing buildings and replace them with parks. Neither is there any way their owners will "volunteer" to make the (supreme) sacrifice.

But suppose the activities decanted from OB to NB are financed by their replacements — i.e. by the new offices that buy up the existing buildings. OB is still full, granted; but it is much better off than before because NB has *started cooking*. Soon NB will reach critical mass and migration patterns will change, taking the pressure off OB.

The problem of generating a viable urban centre within a developing economy is indeed formidable, especially since the employment-generating inputs, really the crux of the problem, are in short supply. Techniques must be found for using some of these inputs over again. Certain inputs are obviously more mobile than others. They are, in that sense, reusable. For instance, dock facilities once set up, cannot be moved. The government, on the other hand, is highly mobile.

Furthermore, in most Third World countries, the State has a high profile indeed, controlling "the commanding heights" of the economy, so that government jobs have a high multiplier effect (estimated at five, in the context of Bombay). If we are to generate new urban growth centres within the limitations of our economy and our resources, we will have to find techniques for re-using key inputs of the urban equation several times over. As soon as a healthy and sustained growth is assured, some of these ingredients must be remarshalled and used again elsewhere. This is like a technique for grafting trees. Or perhaps a better analogy would

A fixed asset . . .

. . . and a moveable one.

be a travelling circus — the government pitches tent every 20 years and generates the process of urban growth; then moves on.

The important thing to remember is that this kind of growth has occurred before. The British really created Bombay, Madras, Calcutta and New Delhi, out of thin air. The Spanish manufactured Lima just to have a port to ship the gold back to Spain. These colonial powers, whom Buckminster Fuller rightly calls "world pirates", were very decisive people. They knew they would have to act quickly and forcefully to keep their empires going. It seems to be much more difficult to get national governments thinking in these terms (the British government is perhaps less decisive about domestic issues today than it was about Imperial matters 50 years ago). Yet it is crucial that the techniques of rapid urbanisation be invented. For within this decade the countries of the Third World must begin to plan their urbanisation patterns as boldly as they plan industrialisation today. (The USSR was, perhaps, the first country to plan industrialisation through a crash programme on a nationwide basis. They were so successful that the first thing any new nation does — after designing the national flag — is set up a commission to plan industrialisation. Unfortunately, Lenin did not attempt restructuring the urban pattern on a national scale, so the new nations do not see that part of the problem.)

Perhaps the most profound planning lessons of all lie not in our textbooks, but in history. How did Bombay become such a great metropolis? There are dozens of suitable bits of coastline in India, so why Bombay? To answer that question, we have to unravel the genetic code, the D.N.A. of Bombay (or Sao Paulo or London). Even today Bombay has an extraordinary vitality — fuelled by its role as the financial capital of India. Fifty years ago Bombay was just another harbour city, with a population of less than a million

Pitching tents and grafting trees.

Fort St. George, Madras, in the 17th Century.

people. Calcutta, on the other hand, was a great metropolis and the real financial capital of the whole sub-continent. But the British, perhaps for reasons of military logistics, preferred Bombay and, with the Reserve Bank Act of 1934, made it the banking centre of India. That was the day Calcutta died (the first lethal blow had already been struck a decade earlier when the Imperial Government moved to New Delhi), and a crucial new ingredient was coded into the double helix that underlies Bombay.

With the flow of migrants into existing centres, the slums and uncontrolled settlements contain an ever larger portion of the urban population: 33% in Karachi and Calcutta, 41% in Brasilia, more than 45% in Bombay, 80% in Buenaventura (Colombia). But this sorry state of affairs need not prevail. Given the political will, the enormous demand in our cities today can be used to advantage. For the very scale of this demand allows the planners to shift their focus to large new contiguous territories — and thus restructure the city in the process.

The rising tide.

If intelligent incentives are provided, decanting existing activities to these new locations can be a viable objective. And if this new land is first socialised and then developed, the resulting increase in land values can help pay for the infrastructure of roads, sewage lines, etc. This has the further advantage of restricting the use of the limited resources of the developing agency to the infrastructure and transport systems alone.

Thus, with a minimal amount of seed money, it should be possible to use the enormous urban growth of the coming decades to help support itself. The concept of self-help housing already exists; there must now come into being the concept of — and the programme for — the self-help city.

8

Scanning the
Options

Searching for a future.

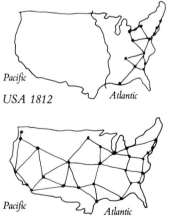

Pacific

USA 1812   *Atlantic*

Pacific

USA 1912   *Atlantic*

The scale of the problem determines the solution. This is the key to the strategies we must develop over the next 25 years. If we succeed in our interventions, we may then be able to *use* this growth to our permanent gain and emerge from the tunnel better off than when we entered. After all, in the past, most cities have grown by continuous, incremental stages. Thus the authorities never perceived the opportunity to "rearrange the scenery". Let us, for instance, turn the clock back to the time when New York had only 1 or 2 million inhabitants. If, at the stage, it had been apparent that it would soon accommodate 10 million people, a lot of basic structural changes might have been not only financially possible but *politically* viable, and New York would be a far more rationally organised city than it is today.

And this in the final analysis, is the advantage of our predicament. That, for the first time in history, we are able to perceive an enormous quantum leap in urban growth; a perception that should prompt us to re-adjust the scenery we've inherited. Intelligently done, this could have staggering geo-political implications. Consider, for instance, the leverage the U.S. gets from an urban structure which spans a continent and connects two oceans. A little over a century ago, the U.S. was dominated

by its eastern seaboard cities — i.e. Boston and New York, etc. — facing only the Atlantic. The reason why that nation can now address the Pacific is that in the interim there has grown a matching set of urban centres along the West Coast — San Francisco, Los Angeles, etc. — and also right across the continent — Detroit, Chicago, Denver. It is an organic interdependent urban structure generated by the enormous population growth that has taken place in the U.S.A. over the last 100 years. Australia, by contrast, was structured to face Britain through its south-eastern ports of Melbourne and Sydney. Although its future lies with its Asian neighbours to the immediate north and west, Australia doesn't have the dynamic population growth necessary to make such urban restructuring possible. Where there's growth, there's hope.

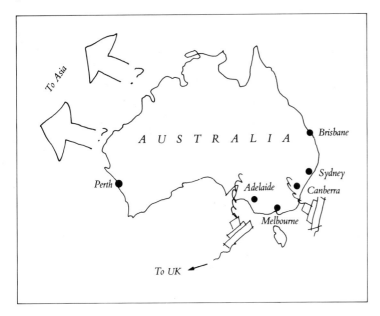

Slow population growth.

This is not to say that population should continue to grow in the Third World. It is merely to emphasise that, despite anything we do, Third World populations will in many cases double before they stabilise ("Enough girl babies have already been born, etc …"). We do not have much choice about that. What we *do* have a choice about is their distribution pattern across the nation, as well as the internal structuring within urban centres. Future generations will certainly hold us accountable if we miss this unique opportunity.

The colossal numbers involved need neither confuse nor intimidate us. True, a single city of 10 million seems unmanageable — but what if the same population were distributed in a poly-centred system of 5 or 6 centres, each of a reasonable size? Such urban structures already exist, for instance in the Bay Area in California where a number of separate centres (San Francisco, Oakland, Marin County) together form one urban system involving over 5 million people, while San Francisco itself has a population of under a million. In the same way, several Dutch cities (Amsterdam, The Hague, Rotterdam) form a single poly-nucleated urban system, each unit of which is on a manageable and human scale. And in India itself, Kanpur, Allahabad, and Lucknow, etc. form one urban system.

These kinds of models are certainly worth examining. In fact it is disquieting to realise how seldom we stop to ponder just how wide open our options might really be. Perhaps, what is needed is not just more towns and cities in the conventional sense, but a new style of community — quasi-urban/quasi-rural — which produces densities high enough to support an educational system and a bus service, yet low enough for each family to keep a buffalo or a goat and a banana tree. In fact if residential densities can be brought down to about 50 households per hectare, it becomes feasible to dispense with central sewage systems and recycle waste matter (both human and animal) to considerable advantage: cooking gas, fertiliser, small vegetable gardens, etc. Under Indian conditions this would have the additional advantage of continuing the pattern of life to which people are accustomed — as though Mahatma Gandhi's vision of a rural India had an almost exact quasi-urban analogue.

Like *gobar* and bio-gas, to us in India, of course, the sun is another great harbinger of the new landscape. In much of the Third World the most cost-effective strategies for harnessing solar energy are not through gadgets such as solar frying pans (expensive to produce and relatively inefficient) but through setting up biological cycles: shallow ponds to grow algae and plants which photosynthesise the solar energy incident on the water and which are then ingested by fish and other higher forms of life and so forth, until we are the final recipients (though of course we in turn must inevitably be consumed in order to continue the cycle!) The employment-generating possibilities of such cycles are considerable, as in a pilot project in New Bombay where it was estimated that not only the building of the ponds would provide additional jobs, but also that the excavated soil could be used to form simple sun-dried brick.

These cycles can establish the economic bases of communities and will of necessity determine their physical pattern — just as today's cities have been generated by the carriage and the automobile. They can constitute a new type of human settlement, using the Third World's unique combination of plentiful sunlight and abundant human labour.

A commune in China.

If and when these settlements come into being, they will bring about two fundamental changes. First, since God's sunlight falls just about equally all over any of these Third World countries, the demographic pattern of population distribution will also follow suit, avoiding the centralisation and the large concentrations inherent in industrialisation. The second consequence follows from this pattern; for in such a world of evenly-distributed self-contained communities the political power structure must change dramatically, since no one will be able to pull a lever in Delhi (or Lagos, or Sao Paulo, or Jakarta) and affect millions of people right across the nation.

Obviously postulating these profoundly important prototypical settlements for the Third World is not merely a question of employment. What we need to conceptualise is the social system, the life-style of the new settlements. After all, the communes of Mao are not just a legal contract binding a certain number of people to harvest together, but really the only political-social-human reality the commune members know — like fish know the water they swim in. It will take an effort of equivalent inventiveness to find the *modus operandi* for these new human settlements.

Vastu-purusha: man as a cosmic being.

In the past, such imaginative conceptualising was seldom lacking. For instance in India since Vedic times, sacred diagrams called *mandalas* have formed the basis of architecture and city planning. These square *mandalas*, sub-divided in prescribed ratios from 1 to 1024 sub-squares, represent the cosmos — no less! The hierarchy they generate forms a matrix for locational decisions — whether of deities in a temple, or of the principle buildings in a city. They make explicit a Platonic ideal of built form which in turn reinforces and stabilises society.

Today such concepts are not in current use, and it would be foolish to think of invoking them unless we also subscribe to the underlying construct of the cosmos they are meant to represent. Still, in a century when science has postulated an ever-expanding universe, it may well be worth our while to consider the modelling of our central beliefs as the basis for structuring our environment.

Temple and kund at Modhera.

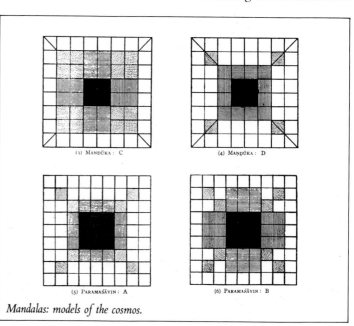

(3) MAṆḌŪKA: C

(4) MAṆḌŪKA: D

(5) PARAMAŚĀYIN: A

(6) PARAMAŚĀYIN: B

Mandalas: models of the cosmos.

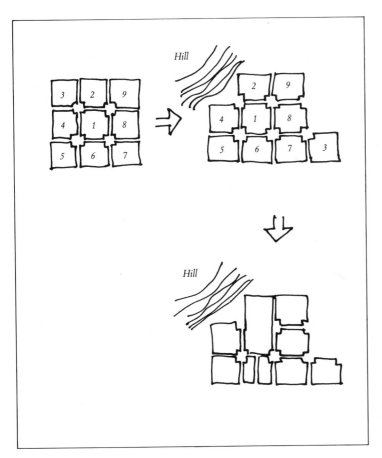

The plan of Jaipur started with the 9-square mandala (an analogue of the planets). Square 3 was displaced by an existing hill and re-appeared next to square 7. Then squares 1 and 2 combined to house the palace.

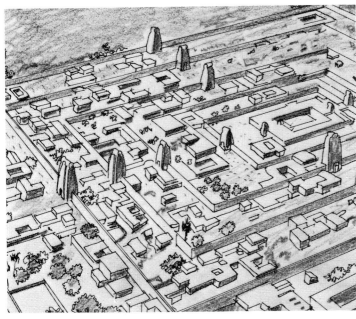

The mandala as temple town: Srirangam, South India.

We must be equally inventive about generating habitat on the micro-scale. There is, for example, little relation between the form of our streets and how we use them. Most side-walks in Bombay are always crowded — with hawkers forcing pedestrians onto the traffic lanes by day, and, as evening falls, with people unfolding their bedding for a night's rest. These night people are not pavement-dwellers, but domestic servants and office boys who keep their belongings in a shared room and use city pavements for sleeping. This pattern allows them to economise on living expenses and maximise the monthly remittances sent back to their villages. What is dismaying is not that they sleep outdoors — on hot sultry nights a more attractive proposition than a crowded airless room — but that they have to do so under unhygienic conditions, with the public walking right amongst (and over!) them. Is there any way in which the city streets and side-walks could respond to their needs?

Modifying Bombay's streets with a line of platforms, 2m wide and 0.5m high, with water taps at 30m intervals. During the day these platforms would be used by hawkers — thus clearing the arcades for pedestrians. In the evening, water from the taps would wash the platforms clean — creating otlas for people to sleep on.

Today:

3M   19M   3M

Proposed Platforms:

Proposed Platforms
2M wide with water taps
at 30M c/c

Daily 9am to 7pm:

Acts as Barrier
between pedestrians
and cars

Hawkers

Nightly 9 pm to 7 am:

Platforms washed at 8 pm
Used by people for
sleeping

3M   2M   15M   2M   15M

Sharing the same aesthetic . . . as opposed to conning the client.

To be involved in these issues, the architect will have to act not as a *prima donna* professional, but one who is willing to donate his energy and his ideas to society. It is a role that has a very important historic precedent. For throughout most of Asia his prototype has been the site *mistri*, an experienced mason/carpenter who helped with the design and construction of the habitat. In the small towns and villages of India, the practice continues today. Owner and *mistri* go together to the site and with a stick scratch on the earth the outline of the building they wish to construct. There is some argument back and forth about the relative advantages of various window positions, stairways, and so forth, but the system works because both builder and user share the same aesthetics. They are both on the same side of the table! It was exactly this kind of equation that produced the great architecture of the past, from Chartres to the Alhambra to Fatehpur-Sikri. (If the architect today cannot convince a client, could he have been able to overrule a Mogul emperor 300 years ago — and survive?)

Today the situation is quite different. Not only has the shared aesthetics evaporated, but the interface has diminished. Only about 10 percent of the population have the resources to commission the kind of buildings the academically trained architect has learned to design — and only a tenth of *them* would think of engaging him. The others would appoint a civil engineer, or perhaps go directly to a contractor. So there you have the modern architect's interface with society: all of 1 percent. This figure represents the people who commission the office buildings, apartments, luxury hotels, factories and houses that make up the bulk of the architect's practice. The situation is not of his making; it merely reflects the grotesque inequality within society itself.

But it is of course the poor whose needs are the most desperate. Today in Rio or Lagos or Calcutta, there are millions living in illegal squatter colonies. Is the architect, with his highly specialised skills, going to find a way to be of any relevance to them?

Why do we build this?. . .

. . . when this already exists: low-energy high-visual habitat in Rajasthan

Unfortunately, even among those architects who have the social conscience to want to reach out to the poor, many are really a-visual — in some cases, in fact, belligerently *anti-visual* — rejoicing (as they move among the poor like Florence Nightingale among the wounded) in the acres of ugliness/goodness of it all. What these communities need is not just our compassion, but our professional, (i.e. visual and topological) skills. Without these, the squatter colonies will turn out to be nightmares — proliferating, over the next two decades, on a scale which boggles the mind. In turn, they will maim

House-decoration in New Bombay ...   ... and Udaipur.

whole generations of Third World children, condemned to grow up in such environments.

We cannot just trust to luck and a blind faith in humanity. For every Mykonos history has created, there are ten other depressing towns. The stunningly beautiful handicraft and weaving of certain societies are the fortunate result of a cumulative process, spread out over many decades, with each generation making marginal improvements to the end product. Without the benefit of such a heritage to provide context, people often opt for ugly things — the principle of Miami Beach.

If we want to increase the probability of winding up with something as beautiful as Udaipur, then strategies for sites-and-services will have to be programmed accordingly. Perhaps by giving extra weightage to those residents who are visually sensitive, so as to hasten the process? (In a self-help scheme in New Bombay for instance, folk artists were brought in as catalysts to work with the householders.)

To value the visual component, so obviously present in traditional habitat, is not to join the epicene enthusiasms of today's fashionable eclecticism. Far from it. We must understand our past well enough to value it — yet also well enough to know why (and how) it must be changed. Architecture is not just a reinforcement of existing values — social, political, economic. On the contrary, it should open new doors — to new aspirations.

To reach the millions who lie on the pavements and in the shanty towns is to get involved in a whole new series of issues, issues to which we must bring the instincts and the skills of the architect. I emphasise this again, because too often, in entering this arena, the architect leaves the best of himself behind. Hence the stultifying sites-and-services schemes, all "justified" on the grounds that an aesthetic sense is something the poor cannot afford.

Nothing, of course, is further from the truth! Improving the habitat needs visual skills. The poor have always understood this. With one stroke of a pink brush, a Mexican craftsman transforms a clay pot. It costs him nothing, but it can change your life. It is not a coincidence that the best handicraft comes from the poorest countries of this world — Nepal, Mexico, India. And the Arab had only the simplest tools — mud and sky — so he *had* to be inventive. In the process he produced some of the most glorious oasis towns (*low-energy, high-visual!*) the world has ever seen.

Clay pots.

Jaisalmer.

Udaipur.

Banni.

From Polynesian islands to Mediterranean hill-towns to the jungles of Assam, for thousands of years people have been building incredibly beautiful habitat. In fact, if we look at all the fashionable concerns of environmentalists today — balanced eco-systems, re-cycling of waste products, appropriate life-styles, indigenous tech-nology — we find that the people of the Third World already have it all. Ironically enough, that's the wonderful thing about the Third World: *there is no shortage of housing*. What there is a shortage of, most definitely, is the *urban context* in which these marvellously inventive solutions are viable.

This then is our prime responsibility: *to help generate that urban context*.

Mykonos.

Hyderabad, Sind.

Architecture as an agent of change... which is why a leader like Mahatma Gandhi is called the Architect of the Nation. Not the Engineer, nor the Dentist, nor the Historian. But the Architect — the generalist who speculates on how the pieces can fit together in more advantageous ways. One who is concerned with *what well might be*.

To do this in the context of the Third World the architect must have the courage to face very disturbing issues. For what is your moral right to decide for ten thousand, for a hundred thousand, for two million people? Then again, what is the moral advantage in not acting, in merely watching passively the slow degradation of life all around?

The dilemma is cruel: to act, or not to act. On the one hand, the dangers of Fascism, on the other the paralysis of Hamlet. It is a profoundly disturbing issue, one which will define the key moral values of the first half of the 21st century. In this the role of the architect will be central: can he really understand another's aspirations? In the 1960s, when European hippies first came to Bombay, a lot of rich Indians complained bitterly about them. At dinner parties they would refer to those "terrible, dirty people, with lice in their hair, lying on the pavements begging". In response one would say, "It doesn't bother you when you see an Indian under those conditions. Why do you get so upset when you see a European?" Finally, a friend gave me the answer: "Naturally a rich Indian goes berserk when he drives his Mercedes and sees a hippie. The hippie is signalling him a message: *I'm coming from where you're going — and it's not worth going there.* That upsets him terribly."

But, come to think of it, surely the message can work the other way around as well! The hippie should realise that the Indian in

Hippies doing their thing.

116

The Metropolis as mirage.

his Mercedes, gross as he may be, is also sending a message, in fact the very same one: I'M COMING FROM WHERE YOU'RE GOING.

We are but ships that pass in the night — as this photograph of Bombay's skyline illustrates so poignantly. Silhouetted in the foreground are the squatters. Behind them rises a group of new skyscrapers. To us the buildings are ugly and deplorable — but to them they form the surreal mythic image of the city, which they yearn for, but which they may never attain.

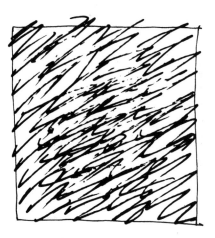

A twentieth century composer — I think it was Hindemith — was once asked the mind-boggling question: How do you compose your music? He gave an astonishingly evocative yet precise answer: "It is like looking out of a window into the black night of a thunderstorm. Suddenly there is a flash of lighting, illuminating the entire landscape. In that one split second, one has seen everything — and nothing." What is called composition is the patient re-creation of that landscape, stone by stone, tree by tree.

Will the cities of the Third World survive the next few decades? The answer may well depend on whether or not we have the perceptiveness to search out and recognise the stones and trees . . . as they gradually coalesce into the new landscape.

PHOTO CREDITS

p. 10, 11: Migrants, Rosso, Mauritania; Kamran Adlé/AKAA.

p. 12: Icon of the 20th Century ...; Imperial War Museum, London.

p. 13: The human condition: "Bicycle thieves", by De Sica; L'Avant Scene Editions, Paris.

p. 16: Sharing a cup of tea; Joseph St. Anne.

p. 20: The will to survive; The Illustrated London News Picture Library, London.

p. 21: Trying to influence family size – and failing; The Photo Source, London

p. 28: Elephanta caves; Praful C. Patel.

p. 36: Open space in New Delhi; Government of India Tourist Office, Singapore.

p. 37: ... at the expense of squalor in the old city; CRY – Child Relief and You, Bombay, India.

p. 37: The perfect trade-off between covered and open-to-sky space: the hillside town of Saana, Yemen; Christopher Little/AKAA.

p. 38: A courtyard in Marrakesh, Morocco; Serge Santelli.

p. 45: Strolling along a Parisian boulevard; Brian B. Taylor.

p. 49: Row houses in London; H-U Khan.

p. 52: Locked into equality; National Capital Development Commission, Australia.

p. 54: ...or a poor one; Kulbhushan Jain.

p. 55: Housing at Belapur; Joseph St. Anne.

p. 61: A hierarchy of spaces; Joseph St. Anne.

p. 64: Getting to work in China; Joan Lebold Cohen.

p. 66: The spread of New Delhi defies efficient public transport; Medd Collection, Cambridge South Asian Archive.

p. 67: Bombay: Morning rush hour; Sandra Lousada.

p. 77: Ganpathi festival; Government of India Tourist Office, Singapore.

p. 79: Indian nurses in the Gulf; CRY – Child Relief and You, Bombay, India.

p. 80: Parisians discussing their monarch; Documentation Photographique de la Reunion des Musees Nationaux, Paris.

p. 80: Energy and enthusiasm, Multan, Pakistan; Jacques Bétant/AKAA.

p. 82: Calcutta in the 1880s'; reproduced from Splendours in the Raj by Philip Davis, and published by John Murray, London.

p. 82: ...and a hundred years later; Raghubir Singh, Paris.

p. 84: ... but ah, Manhattan; Ismail Serageldin.

p. 86: The power and the glory ... of Big Arithmetic; reproduced with the permission of Aperture Foundations, Inc.

p. 87: Workers' housing by Walter Gropius; Brian B. Taylor

p. 87: Cloning suburban houses ...; Landslides, Boston, USA.

p. 87: ... and high-rise towers; Hong Kong Tourist Association, Singapore.

p. 94: New Delhi government as an agent of change; John T. Panikar.

p. 100: A fixed asset...; CRY – Child Relief and You, Bombay, India.

p. 100: ... and a moveable one; reproduced from le Corbusier, Oeuvre Complet 1957–1965, Verlag fur Architektur, Artemis Zurich, 1965.

p. 101: Fort St George, Madras, in the 17th Century; reproduced from Splendours of the Raj by Philip Davis and published by John Murray, London.

p. 102: The rising tide; CRY – Child Relief and You, Bombay, India.

p. 104: Searching for a future; CRY– Child Relief and You, Bombay, India.

p. 107: A commune in China; Christopher Little/AKAA.

p. 108: Temple and kund at Modhera; Ram Rahman.

p. 108: Mandalas: models of the cosmos; Motilal Banarsidass Publishers.

p. 111: Sharing the same aesthetic; Government of India Tourist Office, Singapore.

p. 112: ... when this already exists; Kulbhushan Jain.

p. 114: Clay pots; Kamran Adlé/AKAA.

p. 115: Banni; Kulbhushan Jain.

p. 115: Hyderabad, Sind; Martin Hurlimann, Zurich.

p. 116: Hippies doing their thing; Joseph St. Anne.

p. 117: The Metropolis as mirage; Joseph St. Anne.